FROM TYNE TO TSAR

A personal account of the maiden voyage of
SS Salient from South Shields to the Black Sea and
back via Genoa, Constantinople, Dartmouth and
Rotterdam, March–June, 1905

Arthur McClelland

**University of
Sunderland Press**

© Grigor McClelland

ISBN 1-873757-21-2
ISBN 978-1-873757-21-5

First Published 2007

Cover Design: Tim Murphy, Bradley O'Mahoney Creative Ltd.
Photograph inserts: page design by Tommy Anderson, BASELINE>SHIFT; image enhancement by SVW Simon Veit-Wilson Photography Ltd. www.veit-wilson.co.uk

Published in Great Britain by
The University of Sunderland Press
in association with Business Education Publishers Limited
The Teleport
Doxford International
Sunderland
SR3 3XD

Tel: 0191 5252410
Fax: 0191 5201815
http://www.grs.sund.ac.uk/sup/home.asp

All rights reserved. No part of this publication may be reproduced, stored in a retrieval system, or transmitted, in any form or by any means, electronic, mechanical, photocopying, recording or otherwise, without the prior permission of the *University of Sunderland Press.*

British Cataloguing-in-Publications Data
A catalogue record for this book is available from the British Library

Printed in Great Britain by The Alden Group Oxford.

Contents

FOREWORD *by Sir Ian Wrigglesworth* — ix
Editor's note — xi
Map of the voyage — xiv
Introduction — xv

CHAPTER ONE
From South Shields to Genoa: *8-24 March* — 1

Signing on. Sea trials. Seasickness. Head winds – a Jonah on board? Heavy weather through the Bay of Biscay – fiddles for meals. Entering the Mediterranean. Past the Balearics and along the Riviera to Genoa. A race to get in. Customs. The German Empress.

CHAPTER TWO
Exploring Genoa: *25 March to 6 April* — 15

The cathedral. A 'scrumptious repast'. The king's palace. Genoa v. Milan at soccer. The Campo Santa cemetery. A 'Strad'. and some Gobelins. The Pallavicini Gardens. Up the funicular. The British Royal Yacht. Schooners at Savona. Old Masters in the Rosso Palace.

CHAPTER THREE
On to the Black Sea: *7-13 April* — 29

Monte Cristo, Stromboli, the Straits of Messina. Down in the engine room. Islands of Greece and Turkey. All hands busy painting. The Dardanelles and the Sea of Marmora. Constantinople from the sea. 'HE SAW THE MASSACRE'. Through the Bosporus. Another of the captain's practical jokes.

CHAPTER FOUR
Ochikoff and Kherson: *14-28 April*   37
Reception at Ochikoff. Up-river to Kherson. Cricket v. *SS Elswick Tower*. Fat Mary the washerwoman. Inquisitive locals. Exploring the market. Ladies on board. Loading grain by hand. A country walk.

CHAPTER FIVE
Nicolaieff and Odessa: *29 April to 6 May*   47
Tsardom detecting Russians on board. Football v. other British ships. A haircut for 7½d. Beekeepers show their hives. Jewish friends at home. Overnight by boat to Odessa. A fine hotel. Odessa's seaside resort. Dinner with the British shipping agent at home. Back in Nicolaieff, more socialising with British, Dutch, Russians. Local cavalry exercises. The Yacht Club. Shops shut for the Czarina's birthday.

CHAPTER SIX
Back to home waters, calling at Constantinople: *7-23 May*   55
The Bosporus. Captain Donaldson the pilot. Santa Sofia. The Sultan's Tombs. The bazaar. The boy who wanted to get away. Crete and other islands. Boat drill. Sicily, Pantalaria, Cape Bon, Gibraltar close up. Cape St. Vincent's new lighthouse (but no girl). 'Coal fever', so I beat the captain at chess, and we divert to Dartmouth.

CHAPTER SEVEN
Dartmouth, Rotterdam, and Tyne: *24 May to 8 June*   67
Longshoremen. Battleships' target practice. The Hook and Rotterdam. Meeting visitors from home. The zoo. The Hague, Scheveningen and the Palace in the Wood. Antwerp via Roosendaal by train, its zoo and museum. On to Brussels. Down to the Hook and across to Flamborough Head. Arriving at Dunston. Reunited with family.

POSTSCRIPT
The diarist's later life   79

APPENDIX I
Westolls the shipowners, and the Black Sea trade   83

APPENDIX II
SS Salient, the ship   87

APPENDIX III
Distances and speeds   93

APPENDIX IV
Currency and prices   97

APPENDIX V
List of characters mentioned by name   99

APPENDIX VI
Other vessels identified   103

APPENDIX VII
Glossary   105

INDEX   109

List of Illustrations

'Merchant Ships in Port',
  watercolour by William Lionel Wyllie (1851-1931)
  courtesy of National Maritime Museum, London (front cover)

Route of the voyage	xiv
Model of the barque *Cotherstone*	xvi
The author's indentures, 1900-1905	xviii
Genoa city centre	18

*Sixteen pages of snaps taken by the author,
and pictures from the web and other sources,
are between pp. 24-25 and between pp. 56-57*

Facsimile of page from the original diary	61
Visits from Rotterdam	70
The author in later life	79
A lorry of the firm in 1921	81
The James Westoll funnel and flag	85
The Plimsoll Line	86
SS *Salient* elevation and plan	88
SS *Salient* crew list for March 1905	91
The author as a young man (back cover)	

Foreword

by Sir Ian Wrigglesworth
Chairman, Port of Tyne Authority

The River Tyne has played an immense role in the history of England. The Romans used the inlet at Jarrow Slake, just upriver from the *SS Salient's* point of departure, as the principal port to the northern frontier of their Empire. The Venerable Bede was based on the banks of the river a short distance away, at St. Paul's Priory, which became the birthplace of the English language. For centuries the Tyne has shipped millions of tons of its most famous export, coal, to all parts of the world, creating vast wealth in the region. The keel men, the pilots, the mariners, the shipbuilders, as well as businessmen, engineers and inventors like Stephenson and Armstrong, all played their part over the centuries in making the Tyne a river known right around the world.

Today some 3,000 ships come to the Tyne each year with around 800,000 passengers on the ferries and cruises. Almost 3.5 million tons of cargo is handled, including nearly half a million Nissan cars.

However, this history and these statistics do not tell the rich personal stories that lie behind all this activity. Arthur McClelland's diary and pictures put a human face to the to-ings and fro-ings on the river, illuminate life on a ship between leaving and returning, and record the experiences of an eager young man ashore in four utterly different countries. They remind us what interesting, exciting and dangerous activities are linked to this highway to and from the sea. The diarist must have been one of the first young people to embark on what has now become a commonplace, namely the 'gap year' taken after the completion of education and training. To have done it a century ago, and in such a different way, is remarkable.

The diary records an extraordinary adventure. It makes compelling reading and gives an invaluable insight into life a hundred years ago. Arthur McClelland clearly possessed immense curiosity, and a boldness which was later reflected in his creation of a major regional business.

With this publication his personal diary can be read by all of us. His son, Professor Grigor McClelland, has been able to track down and present a wealth of background and explanatory material. I am sure many people, in the North East and elsewhere, will find it a fascinating narrative.

2 November 2006

Editor's note

Editing of the text itself has been extremely light. The original seems to have been written flowingly and at some speed, so for ease of reading occasional paragraph breaks and commas have been inserted, and single-digit numerals changed to words. When the diary was written (and dated) on the day following the events recorded, the date has been moved so that all dates cover the events of the day, not when they were recorded. Chapter breaks, headings and summaries have been added.

Additional explanatory and background material takes three forms. First, where only a few words are needed, they are inserted in the text, in italics within square brackets. Secondly, usually where only a few lines are needed, there are footnotes on the same page.

Thirdly, at the end of the diary, a Postscript summarises the diarist's later life. This is followed by longer notes on the shipping company, on the ship, on distances and speeds, and on prices ashore. There are also lists of characters and of other vessels mentioned in the diary, and a glossary. Any word or phrase in the glossary, on its first or sole appearance in the text, is italicised and underlined.

Occasional references are made in the appropriate places to published material consulted and used. However, the principal sources for the editorial additions have been Google, Wikipedia, and above all the World Wide Web, invented in 1990 by Tim Berners-Lee and Robert Cailliau, to whom basic credit should be given.

The author took photographs, and developed and printed them on the voyage. Despite one calamity (p. 29), fifty remain and most of these are reproduced, with captions usually drawn from the diary itself. Other contemporary photographs and facsimiles are included.

The original diary was transcribed into typescript by Mrs. Clare Macara (now Mrs. Clare Lambert) in the 1970s. This was not always an easy task (it is one of the easier manuscript pages that is reproduced on p. 61), and particular thanks are therefore due to her.

I am most grateful also to a number of people involved in this publication. To Sir Ian Wrigglesworth, Chairman of the Port of Tyne Authority, for contributing the Foreword. To Professor Tony Hepburn of the University of Sunderland and of the University Press for commending the project to the Board and for encouragement and help in many ways, including contributing the notes at the start of Chapters Two, Four, and Five and many other notes on the shore visits. To staff at Business Education Publishers for conversion of the typescript and graphics into the book. To Richard Keys for much background information, for responding to multitudinous questions, and for pointing me to sources. To Alfred Roddenby for material about the *Salient* and Westolls, including parts of his own forthcoming history of the company. To Maureen Callcott for encouragement and introductions. To staff at the Tyne and Wear Archives Service and at the Discovery Museum in Newcastle, and to a number of others who have responded helpfully and cordially to phone or email queries. Finally, to my wife Caroline Spence for calmly tolerating yet more of my hours spent at the keyboard.

Grigor McClelland

To the diarist's descendants

Dirty British coaster with a salt-caked smoke stack
Butting through the Channel in the mad March days,
With a cargo of Tyne coal ....
John Masefield, 1878-1967

[*SS Reliant* wasn't just a coaster and it didn't have the other cargo such as 'cheap tin trays', but 'coal dust was everywhere' when it discharged Tyne coal at Genoa, and its smoke stack was doubtless salt-caked after it had butted through the Channel – and the Bay of Biscay – in high winds and waves.]

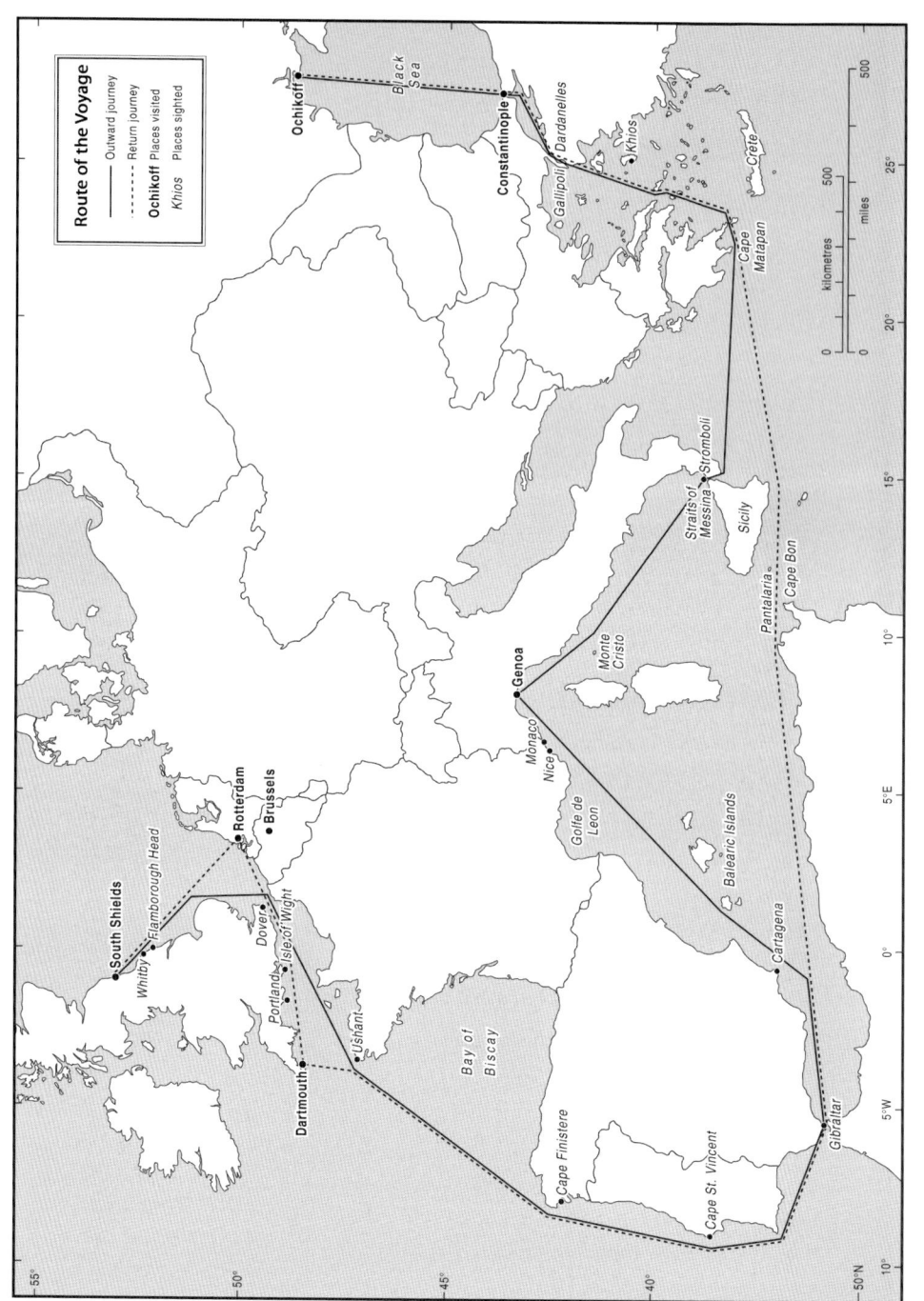

Introduction

It was an unusual 21st birthday present for Arthur McClelland from his parents, to be a passenger on the maiden voyage of the cargo steam ship *SS Salient*, from South Shields to Genoa and then on to the Black Sea. But there are clues to why it might have been chosen. The family lived in Sunderland, then claimed to be the shipbuilding capital of the world, where the *Salient* had just been built. The two younger brothers were studying or to study naval architecture and marine engineering. Although Arthur had already, in his father's footsteps, committed his career to food distribution, he was close to them and shared their interests.

Moreover, he had just completed his apprenticeship, with the grocers Pumphrey & Carrick Watson of Blackett Street and the Cloth Market, Newcastle. That had been five years of hard work for long hours with short holidays (see p.xviii). In the following two decades and more he would also, in a favourite phrase of his from Milton, 'live laborious days'. At this break point, a long sea voyage might have seemed a perfect opportunity to rest and relax, and enjoy a totally different environment. It turned out, as mentioned in the Foreword, to be a shorter version of our contemporary 'gap year', or (given the time ashore, and the sights of the ports and neighbouring towns visited) a sort of poor man's version of the 'grand tour' so much the vogue in the eighteenth century.

Another connection with shipping was that Arthur's father, Andrew Penman McClelland, was a partner in Joshua Wilson & Brothers (JWB), a prominent local firm of importers and wholesalers in groceries and provisions. Founded in 1761, it had had its own fleet of barques, carrying out mixed cargoes and bringing back

Russian, Baltic and Dutch produce, and tea from the far east. Its offices and warehouse were in Lombard Street, near the docks. In 1905 Andrew had been 37 years with the firm, including his apprenticeship, and nearly eight years a partner.

Model of the barque Cotherstone, one of JWB's fleet

As is evident from the diary, Arthur found great interest and enjoyment in the experience. It is a notebook of 248 lined pages (of which the diary occupied 168), measuring 8" by 5", with a cherry-red limp leather cover, bought from R. Ward & Sons of High Bridge, Newcastle. Parts were written in pencil and parts in ink (see facsimile on p. 61). For some reason – perhaps modesty about a youthful literary endeavour – he never mentioned the diary to me, his only child, and I learnt of its existence only after his death. But the memory of the voyage remained with him throughout his life, and he often talked about it.

The captain had clearly made a great impression on him. They played many games of chess together, the captain being the better player. The captain pronounced horizon, 'horrizon' with a short 'i', which Arthur affected to believe must be correct since the captain 'spent all day looking at it'. At one meal, for the captain and the two passengers, there was a jam roly-poly as pudding. According to Arthur, the captain asked him 'Do you like the end?' Since an end would have the least jam in it, the reply was, honestly, 'No', whereupon the captain cut it in two, giving one half to the other passenger and the other to himself. I cannot say whether this story is true, apocryphal, or the exaggeration of a brief tease; but the diary does record several examples of the captain's harmless practical jokes.

The voyage took place just over a hundred years ago. It was the heyday of the British merchant marine, and the *Salient* encountered many other British ships, some from the same line, which had agents in the ports visited. But rail travel had become well established, and one senior member of the line visited the *Salient* in Genoa, having travelled overland. The telegraph was also in use, but for ships' companies, docking at foreign ports was the time for receiving British newspapers and accumulated mail from home – and posting letters and cards.

It was also the age of coal. We get a picture of the effects of the funnels belching out black smoke, the tonnage consumed by another ship when moving at 19 knots, and the 'coal fever' which led to an unscheduled call at Dartmouth on the way to Rotterdam. We learn also that such a steamer had to be able to carry out maintenance, running repairs and improvements involving a variety of practical skills which needed to be represented in its crew (see Crew List, p. 91).

The history of the subsequent century was of course unknown to the diarist and his contemporaries, though it is hard now to realise that such places as Gallipoli and the Dardanelles had none of the resonance those names conveyed to generations after 1915. Russia was under the Tsars (and for the visitor appears to have fully matched the bureaucracy of later regimes). Odessa had still to play its part in the 1905 revolution a month or two later. Constantinople was still the capital of the sprawling Ottoman empire. The German empress who visited Genoa was the wife of 'Kaiser Bill', and the British queen who also visited there was Alexandra, wife of Edward VII (see Pl.21 and 25).

There are references to customs and entry controls, and at one point to risks after dark, but in general the reader is struck by the freedom with which the young author was able to explore ports and their environs in Italy, Russia, Turkey, Holland and Belgium, and to transact with their officials and local inhabitants, even with minimum knowledge of their language. Today the EU has brought down barriers, but one is reminded that the object of Ernest Bevin's foreign policy in 1945, to be able to 'go to Victoria station and buy a ticket to anywhere I please', was based on long folk memory.

The author's Indentures, 1900-05

The Diary

March-June 1905

ONE

From South Shields to Genoa
8–24 March

Signing on. Sea trials. Seasickness. Head winds – a Jonah on board? Heavy weather through Bay of Biscay – fiddles for meals. Entering the Mediterranean. Past the Balearics and along the Riviera to Genoa. A race to get in. Customs. The German Empress.

8 MARCH Wednesday. To start at the beginning let me tell you how I signed on. I went with Captain Nicholson [*see p. 99*] to the South Shields offices at 10 o'clock on Wednesday morning and after an hour wait, most of our crew turned up and we signed on. The Shipping Office[1] is a large oblong room along which runs a counter. In front of the counter are three pens and in these the men gather together, with the master outside near the desk. The clerk puts down name and address, etc., and, after some bargaining, the wage. He then calls out the rules. The men show their discharge books and then sign, the captain giving <u>advance notes</u> [*see Glossary, p. 105*]. The 2nd Mate, 3rd Engineer, Steward and others were there. After we came out I walked up

---

1. This would be the 'Signing-on Office', officially administered and accommodated in the Customs House (now an arts centre) at the Mill Dam, a street bordering some of the quays. See Pl. 2.

with the 2nd Mate, Alf Alderson, to the station and he promised to bring his sextant over from Sunderland. We had to be aboard that night. I went up to Newcastle to bid farewell to my old shop-mates.[2]

At night Willie, Jack [*his two younger brothers*], father and self came over with the luggage and with the help of a small though useful boy found the ship and deposited our luggage. Everything however was in confusion, rooms locked up and steward away and no prospect of starting. So we all went home.

9 MARCH Thursday. I went over by 12.20 train promising to telephone if boat sailed by the afternoon tide. However it was still far from loaded so I came back and went for the last time with father by the 9.20.

He talked a little with the other passenger who we now met, a Mr. Cummings with some connection with the grocery trade and a robust, cheerful and sociable old man. After setting father off I returned and after a stroll round the deck found the captain had arrived with half a dozen others who were to participate in the morning trials, compass adjustments etc.

We all sat round then and had supper from an immense and tender round of beef and large ham. After, everybody sat round, smoked and yarned and I fully enjoyed myself listening to their excruciating tales. One man, Mr. Meldrum, especially distinguished himself. A stout comfortable man with a stiff white torpedo beard and shaven cheeks and a Tyneside accent [*as distinct, probably, from a Sunderland or Wearside accent*].

---

2. At Pumphrey & Carrick Watson – see p.xv.

10 MARCH   Friday. I start writing this diary on Friday morning, the ship steaming up and down the measured mile[3] for trials.

About 1.30 Mr. Cummings and self turned in and slept as well as we could which, however, might have been better for coals were shooting in to the hold very near us[4] with a hiss and banging etc. for some time. I got a fair amount of sleep, however, and rose refreshed at 7.30. The boat had left the Tyne about 5 o'clock, a fact I noticed but was too sleepy and comfortable to get up and witness. From getting outside till breakfast time compasses were being adjusted and then two left us on a tug and we had breakfast, chops and steaks. I had a nice chop and enjoyed it thoroughly.

Although there is a gale of wind it is from the west and the ship in consequence has hardly any motion although the wind catching the tops of waves drowns the lower decks. We, on the lee side under the bridge, are well sheltered from the gale and enjoy the full speed steam very much. After this she does a half speed course and is now doing a 50 revol,[5] the slowest. The course is near St. Mary's Island and she is now on her last trip.

A tugboat took off the trial trippers to the unfeigned delight of the steward who found them rather a handful for one. We then proceeded on our way, steadily steaming south. The wind being N.W. caught us on the quarter and both assisted our sailing and ensured a calm sea. The wind was cold. Mr. Cummings and I spent the day between the cabin and the deck under the bridge, which was very sheltered and one saw the view. In this way we

3. The measured mile (6080 feet, or 1.52 statute (land) miles) in this case was between lines indicated by two pairs of beacons, one pair (posts still to be seen) at Cullercoats and one at Crag Point, SE of Seaton Sluice. The two lines pointed a little north of east, so the ship's course was 160 or 340 degrees from north.
4. It was quite common for a ship to be loaded before undergoing trials, but the South Shields *staithes* were also at Mill Dam, and with them the *Salient's* holds could have been fully loaded overnight. In the 1920s the Dunston staithes (still standing and said to be the largest wooden structure in Europe) loaded 140,000 tons of coal a week.
5. Propeller revolutions per minute. The design speed was 62 rpm (see p. 89).

watched Marsden, Sunderland, Seaham and Whitby go by before dark and about 7.30 Flamborough Head was announced. The wind had gone down however and a slight mist arisen. For *dinner* we had soup, meat and potatoes and an apple each and for *tea* fish.

The captain is kind and quiet. He says for the first day or two he feels leaving home. He spoke of his daughter who is a good singer, his own musical tastes etc. Twice the engines stopped through some slight occurrence in the engine room, such things happening frequently on new ships. The captain is pleased with the boat, which certainly goes very steadily. The steward is a handy man and is surgeon as well. He had two calls on his skill, one of the boys falling from the bridge to the deck and cutting open his head and one engineer getting a slight hurt.

I have been reading *Rome* by Zola.

11 MARCH Saturday. My first night at sea was a good one, eleven hours sleep. After breakfast (sausage) we again paraded the lower bridge and read in the saloon at intervals and sighted the Cross Sands lightship[6] about 10.30. Off these sands the swell is heavy and we ship some water. It also made me squeamish and the Company saved my dinner with the exception of the soup and some bread, for the steak pie finished me. I was not sick, however, and laid down and slept most of the afternoon and felt better as we got past the sands and reached calmer water. The Irish stew for tea did not tempt me and I only had brown bread. The sky has been overcast all day and it is pleasanter by the fire than in the cutting wind. We sighted some of the fishing fleet, which reminds me when doing our trials we saw a torpedo boat doing hers and a very fine sight it was.

---

6. About 10 miles off the East Anglian coast. The previous January, signal guns from the lightship had prompted the launch of the lifeboat from Gorleston (four miles south of Great Yarmouth).

ONE   From South Shields to Genoa   5

The captain has a busy time and sleeps during the day. Tonight we are passing the Goodwins[7] and tomorrow will encounter the Atlantic unsheltered.

At night I raided the steward's pantry (he had gone to bed) and cut myself a thick slice of bread and jam.

12 MARCH   Sunday. The morning was dull with a heavy swell and I got up feeling bad. Half a slice of dry brown bread sufficed for my breakfast, ten minutes after which I was sick, about a pint of yellow bile coming up. Throughout the day I lay quiet on the bench in the saloon and had no dinner at all. The sea went down a little and I felt better slightly at tea time and had three or four slices of brown bread and a couple of sweet biscuits for tea.

Later the steward advised me to go on the *poop* as it was a fine night and the wind had gone down. I followed his advice and had an hour on the poop. It was a clear sky, Jupiter and Venus very bright and fine. We were passing the Isle of Wight and the St. Catherine's point light [*pl. 5*] was flashing over the sea. To the right of it were the lights of Ventnor and other towns, which made a very pretty sight. After an hour of this I went on to the lower bridge to record this. One had to watch for a favourable opportunity as the sea kept breaking over the deck. Through the day in fact it broke two ports in the firemen's quarters and a piece of glass cut the face of one of them. On the lower bridge I had a long talk with one of the apprentices who has been in the Company's service 3½ years. He said he was afraid she would be rather a wet ship because of her great length [*see p. 90*]. While up there a wave broke over the bridge and wet my feet so today I have changed linings and stockings. I went to bed at 9.30.

7.   The Goodwin Sands lie six miles off Deal, rounding the North Foreland, a series of shifting sand banks eleven miles by six. They have for centuries been a graveyard of ships, estimated at nearly two thousand. At low tide in summer there is an annual cricket match on the Sands, and cycles and even vehicles driven.

13 MARCH   Monday. Feeling better. This morning is bright and clear but the captain complains of the head wind which has made us only do 60 miles in the night [*at twelve hours, only 4.3 knots; see p. 94*]. I managed to eat some ling and bread for breakfast and after a short rest to let it settle went on deck and spent an hour and a half on the poop. No land is in sight but it is very pleasant watching the waves rush along the sides of the ship and the spray shoot from the stern when it makes a dive down. Seagulls are in evidence especially when the steward throws some refuse overboard. I also watched him changing the meat in the <u>harness casks</u> and putting salt in. This and other things help to pass the time away.

14 MARCH   Tuesday night. The fresh air has entirely put me on my legs again and I have missed no more meals. Yesterday we steamed against head winds and the same today, which is keeping us back a good deal (*see pp. 94-95*). The captain says we must have a Jonah on board and points an accusing finger at me. This seems to be a favourite sea joke for the chief engineer said the same thing. The weather has been getting rougher continually and the lower decks are always awash and occasional waves break over the bridges and the poop. This morning the sun was very bright and nice so I spent all morning on deck, finding plenty to do in keeping my feet and watching the seagulls and the waves coming aboard.

   The sea air makes us very sleepy and I usually turn in a little after 9 o'clock at night and also spend the afternoon in dozing and reading. After tea at 5 o'clock the captain, Mr. Cummings and self read and chat and about 7 the captain goes forward to the bridge and sleeps in the <u>chart house</u>.

   The rolling of the ship makes us have to use *fiddles* for meals. They are not a perfect invention and you have to keep a sharp eye on the dishes. We hold our soup plates in our hands and have solid mugs instead of cups and saucers.

15 MARCH   Wednesday. Tuesday night was stormy and what with the clash and bangs of the screw and the rain, and the sea pouring off the poop over our heads, at first I could not sleep. As I lay awake an extra heavy wave bent the glass port letting in some water. I at once closed the *deadlight* before the ship rolled back, or we might have been flooded out. After this I got to sleep. We had been making no way against the wind, so in the course of the morning the captain stopped the engines until evening and we wallowed in the biggest waves I have ever seen [*see p.95 note 2*]. The sun was out and I spent the morning on deck. After dinner it was dull at times so I lounged about below. Tonight the skipper and I had one game of chess which he won in about six moves and our next game was interrupted by the rolling of the boat so we had to stop.

Our meals today have been more precarious than ever. The captain narrowly escaped getting the soup tureen in his lap, and the cheese entirely eluded us and went skimming on to the floor. The fiddles are only partly useful. It adds zest to the meal. I am sure it will be quite slow without the motion. In fine weather the steward had the table full of plates etc. and when he brought in the soup we knew dinner was ready. Now however only the bare necessities are placed and he says apologetically 'Dinner is ready', and we sit down to about a knife and a spoon each and he then brings in our food piecemeal.

16 MARCH   Thursday. The wind and sea are still as rough as ever and so we make little progress. The mate said while talking to me that this was one of the worst passages of the Bay of Biscay he had ever made. I feel very glad I am not seasick through it all. I ventured along to the bridge today across the extemporised bridges[8] and later went back and got the camera and took some snaps of the waves breaking on to the deck. This kept me busy till dinner time. About 3.30 I went back but despite watching for waves one caught me and wet my feet. The engineers' and apprentices' cabins are full of water, and I can see the captain worries about this. The sun has been

8. Temporary gangways erected between poop or forecastle and bridge, to save crew going down and up stairs and enable them in rough weather to avoid waves. They would have to be removed for cargo handling.

bright all day. After tea we settled down to talk and read, the ship rolling too much for chess. Mr. Cummings admired the captain's beautiful diamond ring (2½ carats). [*A 2½ carat diamond, cut but not mounted, would cost around £60,000 in 2006*]. I suggested he got it by saving a beautiful princess's life. It was evidently for saving someone's life but he would not say. He won't yarn unless it comes naturally into the conversation.

17 MARCH Friday. My birthday and of course I produced my cake for tea and was congratulated on my 21st. The mates mess-room took a large piece and the rest was on our table.

18 MARCH Saturday. Friday was our last day in the bay and was very much like the others and now this morning we are across and in much smoother weather. This morning is rather foggy but we have sighted Cape Finistere [*at the NW corner of Spain, not Finisterre in Brittany*]. About 9 o'clock we <u>heaved the lead</u>. Once out of the bay the sea grew calmer and the wind went down and it is now possible to walk along the deck without getting wet.

19 MARCH Sunday night. Sunday is signalised by no unnecessary work being done. The mates put on their uniforms and get shaved, an example which I followed this afternoon. The men do their washing and hang it out on the deck to dry. The cook treats us to fresh baked little cakes for tea exactly like what we used to get at Ackworth.[9] I find there is some regularity in meals. On Monday, Wednesday and Friday we get Pea Soup and on Sundays Plum Duff (very like Ackworth 'Shinnock'). During the day we had sighted the mountainous parts of the Portuguese coast and pass more ships than usual. There was a very fine sunset about six which we all turned out and watched. After that the

---

9. The Quaker boarding school near Pontefract, in Yorkshire, attended by Arthur and his two brothers. Their parents had joined the Society of Friends as a result of their close association with the Quaker family that owned Joshua Wilson Brothers.

captain and I played chess. He is a good player and shouts out every now and again 'bad move'. Tonight's game was protracted and not so interesting as others. The captain is referring to past diaries and says we are three days late. This morning he feared fog, which came and went every few minutes, but a fresh breeze sprang up and the rest of the day has been very clear. The glasses proved very useful in observing the coast.

20 MARCH   Monday 9.30pm. The wind has veered round and has been astern N.W. and it has been a very mild fresh warm day. In the morning I procured some white enamel from the 1st mate and the captain drew out a large chess board on the saloon table oilcloth and on this we have painted a permanent chess board to accommodate the captain's large chess men. This occupied the morning and afternoon with intervals for rest.

We have been unlucky in passing signal stations and points of interest at night. Cape St. Vincent which we pass very near to was passed last night about 2 o'clock and now we have just passed Gibraltar. It looks very well by moonlight. Just after tea we got our first glimpse of Africa, a high bold headland, and the Spanish coast on the other side. Then came the red lighthouse of Cape Terifa and then we are in the Straights and gradually reach Cape Europa with a white flashing light. The lights of the town and harbour glisten brightly and the great rock looms above. We pass ships much more frequently now, in the afternoon passing a Messageries Maritimes[10] boat and in the Straights a large P. & O. boat (probably). On Sunday night we sighted a stationary ship showing red lights and at first there was some excitement everyone thinking it was a break-down. However it turned out to be a telegraph cable ship.

---

10. La Compagnie des Messageries Maritimes was a French shipping line founded at Marseille in 1849, which specialised in travel between France and her colonies in Asia and the Indian Ocean. Its golden age was between 1871 and 1914.

21 MARCH   Tuesday 9.00pm. After breakfast our chess board was dry so we had a game with the big men. Today has been dull but fine and we have cruised along the Spanish shore. In the morning we passed the Sierra Nevada range of snow capped mountains. Later we saw a fishing fleet, brightly coloured boats with curious lantern sails. In the afternoon we passed Cape Gatta and tonight Carthagena. I spent the afternoon developing[11] and got about five done. After tea another game of chess from 8 to 9. The captain told us of his youth. He was for five years a choir boy in Durham Cathedral and comes from Evesham.

22 MARCH   Wednesday 10.00pm. This morning we have soon lost sight of land and are now out of sight all together. On our right in the morning were the Balearic Isles very high and precipitous looking. An Orient boat, the *Ormuz*, passed close by and I snapped it and as it passed towards England another liner of the same company passed and they saluted each other with their flags. They have black funnels and grey deckhouses and the P. & O. black funnels and white deckhouses. In the morning I did some P. Cs. and fixed them in the afternoon.

We are now in warm and sunny weather though the wind has been inclined to be chilly. The sea is a beautiful blue, very deep in colour, and the foam and back wash from the ship's sides tones it into all shades lighter. As the sun set about 6 o'clock, a golden colour, it coloured the sea a fine orange tint which we all appreciated on our walk after tea. Later on the full moon came up unencumbered with clouds and making a fine silvery track of light along the water while overhead the stars shone out in numbers. I paced the deck a good hour watching this. This was after our game of chess in which the captain easily beat me twice.

---

11. He had evidently brought not only a camera but portable means of developing and printing photographs. The former would have required the exclusion of light whilst the negatives were unloaded and immersed in a liquid solution. The latter would have been by means of a simple wooden frame with a glass plate and metal clamp, holding the negative firmly over light-sensitive paper while it was exposed to daylight for a given time, producing a 'contact print'. (See Postscript, pp. 80-81).

23 MARCH   Thursday 9.00pm. Today has been a quiet uneventful day. After breakfast alternatively walked the deck, read and talked. The captain tells many funny stories and keeps us laughing. One's idea of walking the deck at first was a gentle lounge but the captain's way is better. He walks sharply up and down, hands in pockets and head well up and so gets some exercise. I have therefore altered my gait to this, though it is rather peculiar walking quickly up and down about twelve steps each way. In fine weather officers and sailors wear carpet slippers, leather shod. My shoes come in useful, though if it gets very warm the heat from the decks may come through. We have been today passing through the Gulf of Lyons [*an error: it is Golfe du Lion – the gulf of the lion*] and had fine weather except for a slight swell. It frequently is very rough here, worse than Biscay, with very short lumpy seas so they tell me. Tonight the steward is sealing up all tobacco, matches and salt in view of the customs officers at Genoa.

24 MARCH   Friday. This morning has been the pleasantest so far, bright sunny weather and the Riviera has passed under view. Sailing close to the shore we have watched pass all the famous places like Nice, Monaco, San Remo, etc. They are all very much alike, fine houses with red roofs and yellow walls stuck up the mountain sides and in the valleys and along the sea front. Behind them the mountains covered with trees at the bottom and with clouds about their summits and sometimes higher hills in the distance covered with snow. Along the front runs the railway with trains occasionally passing. Among the houses are fine churches and huge hotels. One monstrous building[12] at San Remo is just building. On the sea are various small yachts.

Three other boats we found this morning all going to Genoa. We are straining every nerve to beat them with engines at full

---

12. Probably the Casino, which was built in 1905, and for which San Remo, the 'capital town of the Italian Riviera', reckons itself to be famous – 'the undisputed realm of green cloth, roulette, and slot machines lovers'.

speed and boilers at full pressure with wisps of steam coming from the safety valve funnels. This in order to get our place first. We have beaten two but the third (in ballast) still is ahead. We are doing 9½ knots. Hatches are uncovered, ropes got out and other things ready for unloading.[13] The brass caps off sounding holes are replaced by wood stoppers and everything valuable placed under lock and key for the Italian dockers are great thieves. They have been known to steal the ports and to unscrew the brass centre piece on the wheel.

About 4.30 we reached Genoa and steamed right across the bay to reach the entrance thus getting a fine view although the sky was dark with clouds. The city reaches up the sides of the hills in the same way as the Riviera towns though it is much bigger. There are very fine buildings all scattered over right up to the top of the hills and it extends as far each way as can be seen. In the entrance of the harbour were three smallish battleships covered with bunting and firing intermittent salutes as we approached. The forts on the hillside replied at intervals making wonderful echoes in the hills behind and all together we had a fine entrance. As we passed the battleship we gracefully dipped our ensign which flew at the stern.[14] On our aft mast flew the house flag [*p. 85*] and on the fore mast the yellow flag[15] asking for the doctor whom we just got, the other boats which we had beaten, arriving later on, having to wait till this morning, which pleased the captain very much.

13. The ropes would be for docking. Hatches would be covered with beams, hatch boards, and normally three layers of tarpaulin. In Genoa coal would have been lifted by land-based cranes, in grabs or in containers which would have to be filled by shovel.
14. It would have been dipped to halfway on the stern mast. The more senior ship would then have responded, restoring the position of its own flag when the two had passed, at which point the other ship would also restore.
15. Indicating 'My ship is healthy. I require free *pratique*' (Q flag of the International Code of Signals).

We steamed right in to the harbour and moored to another ship for the night. Various officials came on board and the Customs Officer sealed up all dutiable articles coffee, salt, tobacco, matches etc. Captain Stephenson, one of those present during the trials, has come overland and he hailed us from the shore in Tyneside dialect '*Salient* Ahoy' and our boat brought him aboard. The Customs kept us from tea till 7.30 which made us very hungry. We all four had a good tea, Irish stew and then Tongue and spent the evening smoking and chatting till 10.30. Our time here is almost exactly[16] one hour ahead of Greenwich Time.

During the evening, mission boats[17] *came off* and a washerwoman to see about washing. While we were getting moored a magnificent two-funnelled yacht [*presumably the SMY Hohenzollern, see pl. 20*] came out with the German Empress, thus explaining the salutes and flags, a light at the mast-head proclaiming royalty to be on board. When the lights of the town showed it looked very fine.

16. Most places had earlier lived with their local solar time, noon being when the sun was at its zenith. This became increasingly awkward as railways and telecommunications improved. In 1884 a conference in Washington DC, with 25 nations represented, adopted the Greenwich meridian as the 'Prime Meridian' of the world – though the French did not adopt it until 1911, and two others abstained at the conference. See also p. 69.
17. Presumably from the local Seamen's Mission, offering welfare. The Genoa Seamen's Institute is mentioned on p. 16.

TWO

Exploring Genoa
25 March to 6 April

The cathedral. A 'scrumptious repast'. The king's palace. Genoa v. Milan at soccer. The Campo Santa cemetery. A 'Strad'. and some Gobelins. The Pallavicini Gardens. Up the funicular. HM the Queen. Schooners at Savona. Old Masters in the Rosso Palace.

The city of Genoa was known as 'la superba' due its magnificent location and its marble palaces, rising from the sea across the slopes of a mountain. It was already an important centre in the early Roman period, and was constituted as a city-republic in the tenth century. During the middle ages the city was in frequent conflict with its rivals in Pisa and Venice. It fell under French rule during Napoleon's time, but after 1815 it became part of the Kingdom of Savoy-Sardinia-Piedmont, governed from Turin until the unification of Italy in 1860-70. At the time of this Diary it was the most important commercial town and seaport in Italy, with a population of about 235,000.

25 MARCH   Saturday. This morning after breakfast we are being taken to the quay to unload where C. and I intend to land and spend the day. We have each got 50 francs[1] from the captain.

Today is our first day ashore and has been a busy one. We were towed to our berth after breakfast and C. and I were soon ashore. We threaded our way between trains of wagons and heaps of coal till we reached the road along which the electric trains run. It is called the Via Milano. Immediately in front of us was the Seaman's Institute to which we went for letters. Mine, however, had been sent aboard so I did not get them till evening when we returned. A lady met us and gave us good information. We bought stamps and borrowed 30 centimes to take us up to town in the cars [*electric streetcars or trams, of which Genoa already had an extensive system*]. Outside again we prepared to catch a car and I jumped on one. C. however could not while it was running so I jumped off. None would stop however it seemed so we walked on some way till one was blocked with a cart and thus got on. Inside of this I asked for the Piazza Caricamento, as directed by the captain and eventually arrived there, fare 15c.

In front of us was the Hotel Franco. We turned up this along the Via Lorenzo and half way up it was the cathedral,[2] in to which we went for a little, while mass was held. There was a fairly large congregation coming in and going out, many wetting their foreheads with holy water. All sorts and conditions of people, dirty workmen, many old and wizened women, and fashionable people as well. Many got hold of loose cane chairs, which they carried about with them as the priest moved about. The cathedral is very fine inside with stained glass windows and with an apse. We soon came out and wandered along. The Seaman's Institute lady told us where to get money changed but we forgot the name of the places and so had to buy something. We decided on

1. About £2 then and worth about £156 today. For this and other currency references, see 'Currency and Prices', p. 97.
2. Cathedral San Lorenzo, begun in the early twelfth century and extended in the fifteenth and sixteenth centuries, including elements of Romanesque, Gothic and Renaissance styles of architecture. The interior had been restored in 1896.

postcards so went in and bought some. We had no difficulty in getting these as they were the principal article of the shop which like most of the others is very small and cramped but I found the name to be Cartolina Postale [*in fact this is the Italian for picture postcard*].

Leaving here with some silver [*the 10 franc piece of that time was gold, though there was also a note, see below*] we reached a fine large square [*probably the Piazza De Ferrari, the centre of social life in Genoa at this time*] which one comes across every now and again as if to make up for the narrow and tortuous streets. An imposing building opposite us we took for the post office as a van stood in front of the door. We entered and found ourselves in a large hall. At one end was a letter box so we went along and entered a small room where stamps were sold, and bought some with a little difficulty not knowing the numerals. From here we strolled along choosing the nicest looking roads along the Via Carlo Felice where I bought a pipe and got some change out of my first 10 franc note. Next we came into another square and along the Via Garibaldi. It was now past 12 o'clock and we began to think about dinner. We looked out for a restaurant and presently found the Hotel Helvitia with a Luncheon Bill on the window, for 2 for 50. In we went and sat down. First came Macaroni au Gratin, a very tasty dish, then Omelette au Mesjebeer [*spelling unclear from MS*], an entree like eggs custard, with kidneys atop. Then Beefsteak with potatoes and fromage and fruits, apples, figs and dates. We finished this scrumptious repast by 1.30 and found ourselves once more in the open. I bought some cigarettes, 10 for 30 cents, at a little shop.

We next walked along a fine street, Via Balbi, and on the right found a fine large entrance something like the town hall entrance.[3] C. walked in and I followed, though thinking we were intruding. Up the stairs was an inner open court with galleries. I went up and asked a stranger if we were allowed here, in English.

---

3. Probably the Palazzo Marcello Durazzo, built by Bart. Banchi in the seventeenth century, with a picture gallery containing works by Van Dyck, Titian, Caravaggio and others.

GENOA city centre. Only a small portion of the port is shown. The *SS Salient* was docked to the west of the NW corner of the plan. On 25 March Arthur and C. came in from there by tram to the terminus loop at the Piazza Caricamento (1). Discs are numbered in the sequence of the places mentioned in the diary.

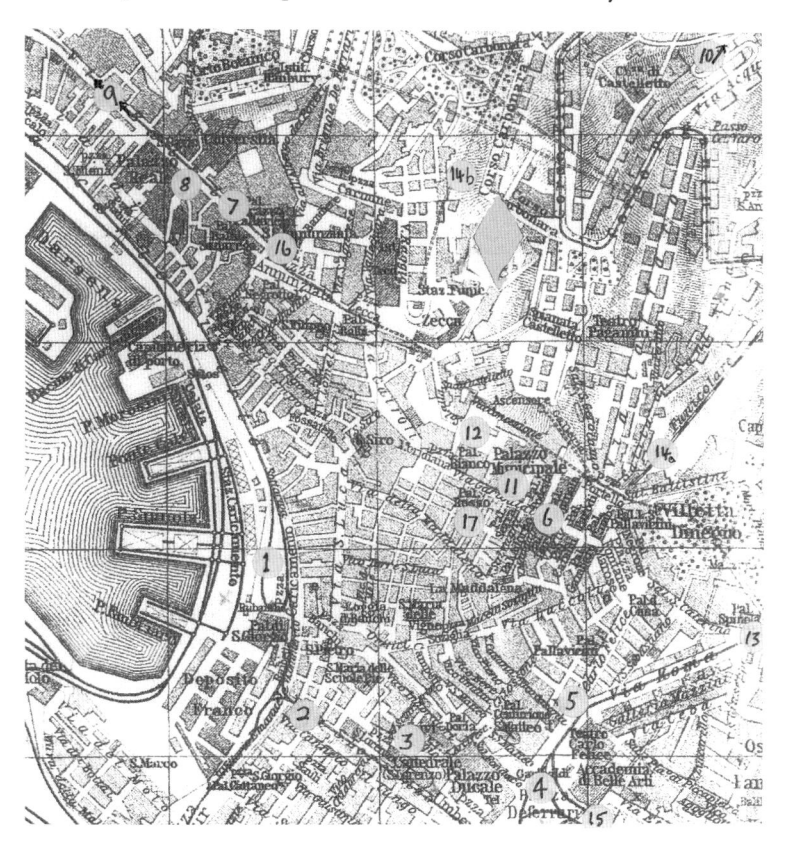

1. Piazza Caricamento
2. Via Lorenzo
3. Cattedrale San Lorenzo
4. Piazza Deferrari
5. Via Carlo Felici
6. Via Garibaldi
7. Via Balbi
8. Palazzo Reale
9. Piazza Acqueverdi
10. Campo Santa Cemetery 1.5km NE
11. Palazzo Municipale
12. Palazzo Blanco
13. Palazza Corvetto
14. Funicola a. and b.
15. Via XX Settembre
16. S. Annunciata
17. Palazzo Rosso

He did not speak it however. He said 'Parlez-vous francais?' I said 'Un peu'. I then said something about 'On permettre nous ici?' He said 'Oui'. I then pointed to the gallery and said 'Et la'. He repeated 'Oui' so we went, after saying 'Merci' and had a walk round. Above was a square gallery through iron gates, at one side there being a fine garden higher up.

After admiring this we went out and a few yards further on found a similar fine entrance on our left. We went in this and were met by a uniformed attendant. We couldn't understand what he said but he took the camera and pointed to a fine stairway of marble up which we went. It was enclosed with glass and after two flights C. sat down on a seat and I went further to see if there was anything. At the top was a landing with three or four men sitting, one of whom rose and unlocked a door inviting me by gesture to enter. I saw there was something in this and went and brought C. up and we entered a large fine room hung with tapestry and pictures. Our guide explained the pictures with a very little English, more French and a lot of unintelligible Italian.

At last I asked where we were and he said 'Palazzo' and pointed to the buttons on his coat which bore a crown and we understood it was the King's Palace [*the Palazzo Reale*]. We saw through the King's suite of rooms, ante-room, bedroom, dressing room and Queen's ditto and their Ballroom, also a fine terrace overlooking the river. There were fine pictures and tapestries, a fine Madonna and some wall painting imitating relief which the guide took great pains to explain. For all this he received a franc and the porter 30 centimes. From here to the Plaza Acqueverdi where is the statue of Christopher Columbus.[4] This was a semi-circular background of fine trees, palms etc. To the left is the station through which we looked and then had a rest under the trees. I then went for a stroll by myself and returned by 4 o'clock when we set out for the ship. We did not know the short cut and

---

4. Erected in 1862. Columbus (1447-1506) was born in the nearby town of Cogoleto.

somehow missed the car, so had to walk right back to P. Caricamento and so back. We just arrived in time for tea. The rest of the evening has been spent on diary and a game of chess.

26 MARCH   Sunday. In the morning we were tired with our heavy day on Saturday so throughout the morning we lounged about the deck and read the newspapers. At 12.30 we had dinner and after that we set out for a football match, Genoa v. Milan.

It was a long way past the Campo Santa and necessitating three cars so we arrived rather late. However only the 2nd Eleven was playing. After them came the 1st Eleven and were finished about 5.45. They were not very good players,[5] about as good as the Ackworth Elevens. They shouted and gesticulated a lot and used all English terms as 'Throw in', 'Goal', 'Corner', 'Fullbacks'. Each game resulted in 1-1.

After the end we came away and waited for a car. They were all, however, complete [*he had evidently picked up the Italian 'completo', full*] so we walked the reverse road in hopes of getting one. All were complete so we went into a Wine House and had black wine and a roll of bread each, wine 40c. a litre and bread 10c. each. The wine was not very nice to my taste, bitter and harsh but it served to wash the dry bread down. Our road lay in a valley between hills, the southern aspect of which was terraced for vines and the valley also grew vines and pear? trees. At every little clump of houses peasants were playing a sort of bowls with stone bowls and either throwing or rolling them [*presumably the Italian bocce or French boules or petanque, then less familiar to the English*]. We here caught a car and went to the terminus and then returned arriving back about 9.15.

---

5. So possibly not Genoa CFC (founded in 1893 by a group of English, to play cricket and football against the crews of visiting English ships, and with Italians excluded until 1897), since in 1898 it became the first ever Italian champions. Nor AC Milan, founded in 1899, also by an Englishman, which won the Italian championship in 1901. Inter Milan was not founded until 1908. Perhaps the use of English on the pitch in this game, before the era of mass communications, may be due to the English founders of those teams.

27 MARCH Monday. We started out about 10 for the Campo Santo cemetery[6] and got there in about an hour along the same road as we went to the football match. As the train goes along, the valley opens out and on the resultant plain and the hill behind it is the cemetery. A high white wall forms the edge, which the cars run past. The entrance is on the left-hand side. Here are stalls and street vendors. We then walked in a fine archway. In front of us was a pathway bordered with box and on either side ran along a colonnade. This colonnade on each side and along the train route forms the border with the hill filling up the back and in regular recesses in these colonnades are fine carvings and set pieces in marble in all imaginable holy subjects forming the tombs of the rich dead. While in the open between the regular box hedges and fine avenues of trees are the ordinary burial places of poorer people. The bodies are cleared out every third year. In the middle of this plain, at the converging of paths, is an enormous statue of St. Mary with a cross at least 40 feet high.

The middle path from here leads to the bottom of the hill where fine marble stairs go up to a round temple and church flanked by colonnades on each side. On each side of the staircase are fine groves of trees and green paths, in fact all over fine trees, palms etc. threw a grateful shade and so many bright coloured flowers that one is never dazzled or wearied with the miles of marble. We inspected all this and then went to the round church [*a rotunda, built in the style of the Pantheon in Rome*]. Inside was splendid. The floor done in different marbles and the roof ornamented with rosettes each of different design. Into this dome the guide sang a few notes with the fine voice so many Italians have and produced a splendid echo. In the middle was the altar and pulpit surrounded by candles and in niches round the sides various Biblical personage, Adam and Eve, Daniel with a lions head, St. Peter and St. Paul etc.

6. A beautiful cemetery about a mile and half from the city, on the banks of the River Bisagno. The Italian nationalist Guiseppe Mazzini (1805-72) is buried there.

I went up further while C. rested and found more gardens above so we determined to explore them after dinner and therefore went out and caught a train further into the country to the Hotel Doria, where by consulting our dictionary we procured a dinner of Macaroni in Corra, Biftick and Lemon and Formaggio and Fruits for 2 francs each. This over, we rested a while and caught the car back for another half hour in the Campo Santo and explored the gardens on the highest part where were more gardens and statues and a fine view over the whole grounds. We then returned, had tea, and set out again about 7.30. We walked about till 8.45 looking at shops and then went to a concert in the Giardine Italiane where there was music and a cinematograph. We had café au lait and got aboard about 11.30.

28 MARCH Tuesday. This morning was dull and after breakfast it rained a little so we set out for the Municipal Buildings[7] where we saw Paginini's Stradivarius violin and various fine tapestries – Gobelin. A few doors to the right brought us to the museum[8] full of curios and paintings. After dinner we walked about and sat in the shade of some trees in the Plaza Corvetto. At tea Captain Ramshaw of the Munificent and Captain Stephenson of the Gladys Royle looked in and spent the evening yarning, Captain Ramshaw making us simply ill with laughter with stories about a Captain Cook, his … neighbour, and admirably … tales.

7. Palazzo del Municipio, a sixteenth century building. Nicolo Paganini, 1784 – 1840, in fact played 'The Cannon', made in 1742 by the Guarneri family of Cremona, and he bequeathed it to Genoa, his home city. It is used by the winner of the Internatonal Paganini Competition. There are far fewer Guarneri violins than Stradivarii, but most virtuoso violinists prefer them.
8. The Palazzo Blanco, built in 1565, restored in 1711 and bequeathed to the city in 1884, when it became a museum, containing some Roman antiquities, some good Flemish paintings, some work by local artists, and an urn containing the ashes of Columbus.

29 MARCH   Wednesday. One of the company's boats, Gladys Royle, has a passenger who has rheumatic feet. I visited him on Wednesday morning and after dinner he arrived and we all went to the Pallavicini Gardens.[9] In the morning C. went to the Consulate to sign on as baker and I did some shopping, buying towels in the Gallerea Mazzini. In the afternoon we started about two by train and went through the tunnel and through the suburbs to Pegli Village on the sea coast [*a small town of about 4,000, popular for sea-bathing at this time*]. Here are the Pallavicini gardens which we entered. My camera was detained and presently the guide started taking us past the Palazzo and around the ornamental gardens with fountains, temples, oriental and Australian trees etc. From the temple of Flora a fine view of Genoa harbour is seen through golden tinted glass. From here we went to a wonderful artificial Grotto where we wandered through passages in the rock, cool and damp, and embarked on a boat on some ornamental waters. The guide took us to the Balancois or swing where water squirts you and to a summer-house approached by winding paths all of which are commanded by squirts of water.

   When we came out we had tea in a restaurant outside the gates, café au lait, toast, sponge cake, rolls and butter, jam and honey and so back to Genoa. At night I went with some engineers and the 1st Mate to a concert at the Seamen's Institute and reached the ship at 11 o'clock.

30 MARCH   Thursday. This morning C. and I went to the town and up the funicular or cable railway[10] which goes to the heights of the town where are nice gardens and houses. After dinner I went to town alone and walked round, and after tea we missed an

---

9. The gardens of the Villa Pallavicini, 7½ miles west of the city, on the railway line to Nice.
10. The city of Genoa clings to the side of steep coastal cliffs, and had several funicular railways at this time.

appointment with Curry, the Gladys Royle passenger, at 6.30 and went to the town. We walked about and had coffee and cakes in a café in XX September Street.[11] I had café au lait and C. had Babiera Wine [*a local Piedmontese wine*] and coffee and cakes. At 9 o'clock we went to the Teatro Verdi[12] which we thought was variety but it turned out to be a three-act play which we could not understand so we came away before the end.

31 MARCH Friday. Today has been quiet and uneventful. I went ashore with the captain and we visited Ramshaw's office and picked up Captain Ramshaw and his passenger and walked to the agent's office, J. White. I left him and soon returned to the ship in time for dinner. After dinner I dozed and then went with some letters to Whites and got news about Nice boat and returned for tea.

After tea C. went ashore and I met him at the Teatro café and had coffee with him there. We then met the captain in the Gallerea Mazzini and were introduced to the widow and returned by devious ways to our ship.

1 APRIL Saturday. We arranged to go to Savona, a country place 20 miles away. We missed our rendezvous at the Principe and so spent another quiet day. I went to White's office to seek C. and found Captain Nicholson and his passenger Curry and went with them to the Municipal to see Paginini's violin

After dinner I stayed aboard, the weather being dull, and went out after tea with the captain and Captain Ramshaw and C, visiting the widow and various marble shops and a restaurant for cafe au lait (whisky for the others) with Paul [*no identification*] and returning to the ship about 11 o'clock.

---

11. Formerly Via Giulia, renamed in honour of the final stage in the unification of Italy, when Rome was joined to the new nation on 20 September 1870.
12. No evidence of a Teatro Verdi in Genoa: the main theatre and opera house was the Teatro Carlo Felice, built in the 1820s.

1. SS Salient. It was usual for such flat-bottomed ships to be allowed to beach at low tide. For detailed description and original drawings, see Appendix II.

2. "After an hour wait, most of our crew turned up and we signed on" (p.1). Outside the Old Customs House, Mill Dam.

3. Paddle tug off Tynemouth.

4. Paddle tug alongside, apparently undergoing inspection, showing paddle box, starboard navigation light, and open bridge or 'pulpit'.

5. "...the St. Catherine's point light was flashing over the sea" (p.5). The lighthouse, around 1900.

6. Looking forward from poop, showing awning framework, derricks and derrick posts, saloon skylight, winch-driven reels.

7. Looking aft from forecastle, showing foremast, ship's code signal flags, and top bridge with open wheelhouse and chartroom below.

8. "The captain is kind and quiet" (p.4). At stern, with stern lamp, red ensign, and pulley to sounding machine.

9. "The sea kept breaking over the deck" (p.5). The ship taking on sea when rolling.

10. "[On Sundays] the men do their washing" (p.8). 'Dhobi' while seated on cover for pipe to poop winch. Facing derrick post, with hatch 9 and poop in the background.

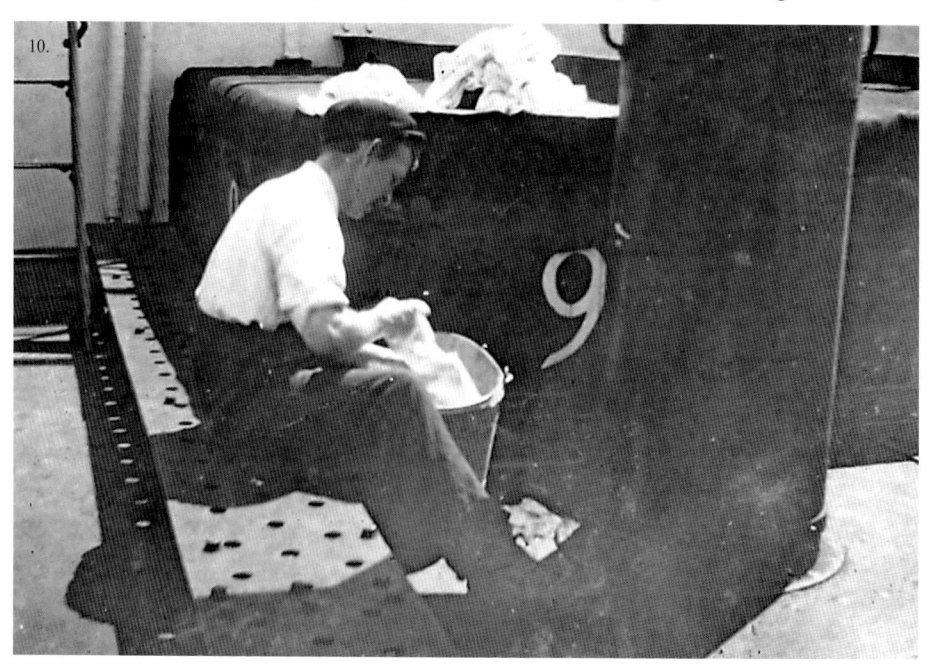

11.

11. "The crew is divided for the two lifeboats" (p.62). This shows the port lifeboat hanging from its davits, its stern being pushed away from its white bed block during boat drill. The forward boats were work boats – without the rope loops alongside.

12. Officer in deck chair, perhaps Captain Stephenson. The double wheel, for manual steering in case of mechanical breakdown, enabled the strength of two men on either side, standing on the non-slip raised grating, to be deployed. "Salient" is written on the cover of the transmission to the rudder.

12.

13. The saloon, with. panelled walls (and doors to cabins), upholstered chairs, coal fire grate, two pictures on a railed shelf above, clock, oil lamp with weighted rope to limit swing, and table (with painted chessboard, see p.9).

14. "After dinner we got out our deck chairs and were soon asleep in the sun" (p.29). The two passengers on the poop.

15. "The 'baker' was dressed in an apron…" (p.38) to facilitate landing in Russia.

16. "As I lay awake an extra heavy wave bent the glass port…" (p.7). The cabin for the two passengers, the younger presumably occupying the upper bunk. Note porthole behind door frame, and electric and paraffin lamps, the latter on gimbals to remain upright.

17, 18. 'The captain and family and chief and his wife and self, after mooring, sailed down again to Tyne dock in the tug boat' (p.76). 17 shows tug boat funnel behind.

18. Shows chief and second engineers.

19. "I took the captain's and officers' photographs" (p.25). The captain (in greatcoat) with mate and second mate.

2 APRIL Sunday. We spent a quiet morning. I took the captain's and officers' photographs. In the afternoon there was a Battle of Flowers at Hervi. I did not go as I could not get anyone else to go as the Queen was expected at 5 o'clock on the yacht.[13] All the British ships strung out their flags. She did not arrive till Monday morning 7 o'clock and left the same time next day. In the evening we all went ashore and sat in the Bavaria Cafe. As it was mid-Lent[14] today all the streets were thronged and cafes full and we saw one girl masquerading [*wearing a mask and fancy costume*].

3 APRIL Monday. We intended to go to Nice in the '*Princess Heinrich*' [*see pl. 30*] for two days. When we arrived at the pay-desk we found it was 35/- each, so gave up the idea and went by train to Savona[15] which is a shipping and seaside place. The most interesting thing was the harbour where were old-fashioned schooners and sailing ships carrying on trade in the manner of two or three hundred years ago. Many carried wine, which was pumped from casks below to casks on the quay with a small hand pump.

After dinner I set out alone for a walk in the lovely country lying to the back of Savona and saw some soldiers drilling. It threatened rain however so I returned and spent the afternoon on the promenade.

4 APRIL Tuesday. In the morning I went and had a hot bath. The Bath was of marble and everything very comfortable – 1

13. Queen Alexandra (1844 – 1925) had married Edward VII in 1863. He was fond of travelling and 1905 saw the first of four cruises he made in the Mediterranean. See Pl. 21.
14. The fourth Sunday in Lent. 'Mothering Sunday' was originally a time for visiting one's 'mother church' in the town one hailed from.
15. Seaport of Roman origin, for centuries a rival of Genoa, later a centre of the Italian iron industry, with foundries, shipbuilding, and railway and engineering workshops.

franc and 10c for soap. We also inspected the Annunciata Church[16] which is the finest in Genoa, of inlaid marble and paintings round the walls in Lady Chapels. The ceiling represented the Passion and the old and new testament. One of the paintings represents a man whose eyes follow one about.

The afternoon went quietly. I got a letter from T. Smith to which I replied. The captain was dining at Ramshaws, so C. and I got the letters at 8.45 and talked with Paul until 11.30 and returned aboard ship. Soon after we arrived the Captain came.

5 APRIL Wednesday. We went ashore with the captain and he sent us with the pilot to inspect the Rosso Palace[17] which has some of the finest pictures in Genoa – Tintoretto, Van Dyck, etc. We got information about a picture, *A Roman Shepherd* by Bruardo Strozzi, of which the captain has bought a copy. Before going aboard we bought ourselves deck chairs at 3 Lira each. We have had some rain during the morning, the last few days being dull. In the afternoon I went a sharp walk via Caricamento Galleria, V Balbi and Principe. C. and captain went to dinner at Ramshaws. I was thus alone and went after tea to the Galleria Mazzini with the 1st Mate Newton. We had coffee and milk and toast at a milk shop and returned about 10 having missed Paul.

6 APRIL Thursday. Our last day at Genoa has been fine, very warm and sunny all day, which has enabled me to get some final photographs. We went ashore with the captain. I paid 3 lira to the Institute and passed the morning in the town. In the afternoon we could not go ashore as we expected to sail every minute, and about 4.30 proceeded to the outer harbour. The

---

16. Santissima Annunziata del Vastato, a late fifteenth century Capuchin church, described as somewhat unfinished and unsightly on the outside, but internally the most sumptuous church in the city.
17. Palazzo Brignole, popularly known as the Palazzo Rosso, from its red face, the largest art gallery in the city, with works by Rubens, Van Dyck, Tintoretto, Titian, Veronese and others.

pilot, captain and I went ashore in a boat and found orders had come to proceed to Odessa, so we immediately returned and are now, 9 o'clock, well on our way. There is a slight swell on, and being light the ship rolls somewhat.

THREE

On to the Black Sea
7-13 April

Monte Cristo, Stromboli, the Straits of Messina. Down in the engine room. Islands of Greece and Turkey. All hands busy painting. The Dardanelles and the Sea of Marmora. Constantinople from the sea. 'HE SAW THE MASSACRE'. Through the Bosporus. Another of the captain's practical jokes.

7 APRIL Friday. On Thursday a finely illuminated Hamburg liner passed us. At breakfast the captain drew my attention to an island on our left, Monte Cristo, rendered famous by the Dumas story. After dinner we got out our deck chairs and were soon asleep in the sun. Suddenly I was awakened by being pulled backwards and finally leaving the chair altogether. It was the captain's doing. He had tied a rope to the chair and, getting on to the deck, pulled. This, unfortunately, broke the back, which he proceeded to mend. After this I started developing and when I finished I had an unfortunate accident. The camera was improperly fastened and 40 films were spoilt including about 30 of Genoa. After tea we had our usual game of chess and went to bed about 10 o'clock.

8 APRIL   Saturday. We have had all day again brilliant fine weather. A slight swell made the ship roll, necessitating the fiddles at meal times. We have enjoyed salad and lettuce since leaving Genoa, which, together with some apples, the captain bought with his own money. Some white paint was brought aft and we have spent the day painting the rails and other parts of the poop, and getting some on our clothes. This passed the day by quickly enough, and about four we caught sight of Stromboli and other islands of this group. We passed very near and could see white steam rising from the crater and, through the glasses, the lava running down. It is a bare brown mountain rising straight from the sea. The lava runs down the North and steepest side. At the N.E. corner is a little promontory. In the bay formed by this and the E. side is the village, protected from the lava by the highest peak of the crater. A considerable number of cottages are scattered about, and through the glasses the terraces of the vineyards can be seen. After tea the captain and I had a very tough game of chess. I captured his queen soon after the start and he got mine soon after.

9 APRIL   Sunday. On Saturday night about 8.30 we entered the Straits of Messina, which are only about a mile wide. An abrupt turn brings us opposite the town, which is sparkling with lights. In the harbour several men-of-war were illuminated with electric light from some festivities, and the whole formed a very pretty sight. Today has been quiet. C. had diarrhoea in the night. In the afternoon I had two games of chess with the captain and one after tea. The sun has been very hot all day.

10 APRIL   Monday. Today a strong head wind has tempered the heat of the sun. During the morning we resumed our painting, doing the starboard and bulwarks of the after deck. About 11 o'clock the captain invited me to see the *tunnel* [*see also p. 88*]. So we descended to the engine room and to the tunnel right along to the end. There was plenty of room and it was lit with electric light. The captain explained the *thrust* and then the Chief took me in hand and showed me the stokehold where the fireman was resting on a bank of coal. Very soon he had to jump up and start coaling, while behind the bunker division an invisible *trimmer* was shovelling coals through. It was fairly hot but was generally hotter, the chief said, as the wind created a good draught. He then explained the engines and answered my numerous questions. Last night they had stopped for six hours owing to an *eccentric rod* bending, the result of overheating. They had also had a slight fire by some leakage of oil getting lit.

After dinner we soon tired of painting and read and watched the coast of Greece, which we are now passing. We passed the island of Cirito [*or Cirigo or Cythera: see note on p. 60*] about 7 o'clock and rounded the 'old man's corner' where a seaman had been so constantly wrecked that he decided to live there; he exhibited a light in his window and passing ships made him presents of provisions. This house still exists but it was too dark for us to see.

11 APRIL Tuesday. We are now proceeding about N. up the side of Greece. On the right we have passed the island of Khios and the Turkish coast and are approaching the Dardanelles. After breakfast we started painting the white part of the Bridge deck. Then I started to paint large numbers on the sides of our nine hatches. This occupied me all day. In the morning a chair arrangement[1] was fitted to the main mast and the Chief Engineer and Second Mate investigated the cause of the electric lights failing up there. The captain would not let me up.

The sea has been very calm with a light wind and the sun very hot. All hands are busy painting. The mate, over the side, touching up the scaffolding rigged on the funnel, which has presented a bad appearance since it was painted red in Genoa and then whitewashed. The whitewash came off and it appeared to have, as Captain Ramshaw said, Scarlet Fever. About the middle of the afternoon we all had a cup of tea, the captain saying we

---

1. Possibly a *bosun's* chair, 'a seat consisting of a short flat board slung from ropes, used to support a man working on the side of a vessel or in its rigging'.

deserved it for working so hard. C. and I both played chess with the captain after tea. Of course he won each game. After that on deck C. and I had an argument on the decadence or otherwise of the modern traveller, as he is always saying 'In my young days they were gentlemen who travelled'. I flatter myself I won, for after pointing out some excellent examples of modern travellers and desiring him to say how his fellows were superior, he said he didn't desire to discuss it any longer.

12 APRIL   Wednesday. We sat up till 11.30 as we were just entering the Dardanelles. We passed Tenedos Island [*see pl. 24*] and reached Shenac.[2] a small town at the entrance. We had here to stop for the night. We then went to bed but were up again this morning at 5.30 when we got *pratique* and proceeded on our way with our Ensign hoisted, as here lays Turkey's fleet, six old and dingy battleships. The Dardanelles remain narrow, although they vary. The land rises gently on each side and seems well cultivated with plenty of little villages and the town of Gallipoli half way.

Presently the Island of Marmora looms ahead. We turn to the left and enter the Sea of Marmora and lose our close sight of land. We are now steaming our fastest to reach Constantinople by sundown so as to get our papers, and we do eleven and over knots per hour. Fast as we go an oil tanker overhauled us, going ½ knot faster. Porpoises abound leaping in twos or threes and once we saw a much bigger shoal. A flock of wild geese passed overhead flying very high and haphazard. We saw many boats, they being crowded together here. Oil tankers to Batoum, our own class of boats and the Turkish small sailing boats called Kengue (Ki-ars) and a Maritime Messageries liner. Today the sky has been clouded, the sun endeavouring to break through. A light wind bears away our smoke but drops it in low black clouds over the calm waters of the sea. This happens to all the ships and it

2. The modern town of Çanakkale, centre of the Chanak crisis of October 1922, when Lloyd George's mishandling of a territorial dispute between Greece and Turkey helped to bring down his government.

presents rather a funny experience. We finish with the Sea of Marmora about 4.45 and enter the Bosporus. The suburbs of Constantinople stretch almost to the end of the Bosporus, which at this end is flat, and we see some fine houses and plenty of trees here. Further on are some factories and we draw near to the city itself about 5.45, cast anchor and get [*are visited by*] two boats and a row boat and a small steamer, the row boat with the ship-chandler [*presumably a shore-based supplier*] and the other with the agent. The captain hurries ashore and gets pratique ten minutes before closing time, which means us missing going ashore. The rowboats are built very narrow and long, like racing boats, and propelled by powerful Turks who go at a great speed. They have to be like this because of the strong current.

We now go on to the appearance of the town. The left bank is the most important and the one we are nearest to. The two shores approach nearer to each other and the Bosporus goes away in a narrower channel. This makes the shape of a funnel, the inside being water and the city lying thickest along the lower end of the tapering part and a short way along the tube. The left bank rises from the water with a gentle slope and is fronted with masonry. Along here right on the edge is the first row of houses and behind these runs, on a masonry embankment, the railway, along which trains are frequently passing and whose whistles are the only noise we hear. Behind here again is a mixed jumble of houses, some large and fine, some very flat with red roofs. All about them are scattered minarets of the shape everyone knows and two mosques are seen, circular buildings covering a large area of ground and rising to a good height but by reason of their great bases looking very solid. One has two minarets and the other a cluster of half a dozen.

This left bank is really an island, Seraglio Island. The Sultana's harem is round the corner and on this island occurred the worst of the massacres[3] of some years ago. Our steward Mr. Brown was

---

3. There had been serious attacks on Armenians by Turks in Constantinople and other parts of the Ottoman Empire in 1894.

here when it happened. He and the captain found their agent shot in the passage-way of his office and with the ship's papers on him. The captain secured them and got away as quickly as possible. On his next voyage they went to Mobile [*the port on Alabama's (limited) coast on the Gulf of Mexico, east of New Orleans*] in the Southern states of America and the captain told the story to someone and next day a page of the local paper was headed in largest type HE SAW THE MASSACRE (pronounced Messy Krey by steward) and subheadings saying how the captain of the *Bencliffe* rescued her papers and escaped amid a storm of bullets.

The indent, formed by Seraglio Island and the mainland meeting, is the harbour and full of ships. To the right of it is the Sultan's brother's palace, a long low marble building with a higher centre-piece and dome, and a promenade along the water's edge. There being no rise or fall of the waters the house can be built close down. As it grows dark the Palace is lit with a row of lights along the promenade and shows the town well up. Another sound greeted our ears which we immediately recognised and which the cook who is passing explains. It is the barking of dogs and comes in volleys from all over the town. The dogs are sacred for having once saved Constantinople, and each pack scavenges its own street and wars with the intruders.

The right bank is very similar but contains one interesting feature, a very large yellow building which was Florence Nightingale's hospital in the Crimea. Also on an island near the shore is a very artistic lighthouse. This side is Scutari and some distance S. of it is the Dog's Isle where extra robed [*??*] dogs are transported as they may not be killed. The town is given a light and fairy-like appearance by the minarets and trees, many of them slender poplars. Every now and then is the pealing of a soft and low toned bell but we listen in vain for the sound of the muezzins calling the faithful to prayer. An excellent service of fast ferry boats runs from Scutari to Constantinople, Clyde boats.

The captain returns aboard with provisions and letters and at ten to eight we leave again and proceed along the Bosporus, here very narrow and lined with houses all well lighted, many of them from the outside, showing their white walls. This presents a beautiful and fairy-like picture as we steam along. We pass the agent Swan's house [*see p. 00*] and toot 'cock a doodle doo' on our whistle, which he replies to by blinking a light. Presently an English pilot passes us and shouts good luck and hopes we brought him some cigars. One very well lighted building is the American college.[4] Here and there are 74 forts of great antiquity and in the city we saw some very old walls. We soon emerge from the Bosporus and are on the Black Sea of which more anon, as after such a long description I deserve a look at the captain's Daily Mails and besides it is 10.30 and bed time for those who rose at 5.30am.

13 APRIL   Thursday. We are now in the middle of the Black Sea, out of sight of all land. Of course we are very sorry to have missed Constantinople but the captain is pleased to have saved time there. In the morning I painted bulwarks and C. cleaned his clothes with turpentine and hung them on the poop to dry. After dinner we read on the poop some Daily Mails the captain bought from Constantinople and presently C. sitting on the <u>Companion</u> Seat dozed over. The captain got a coarse needle and we stuffed his clothes pockets full of rope yarn. Then, leaning over the companion door, tickled him with a string. He kept patting his neck to scare the flies off and we had fits of laughter. Afterwards he woke up and while I held him in conversation the captain sewed the yarn to his pockets and sewed the clothes to his chair and the wheel on which they were hanging. At tea he talked of the severity of the Customs Officials in Russia and said C. must

---

4.   Robert College near Bebek, 'an impressive edifice dominating the narrowest part of the Bosporus', built in the 1860s by its first president, Cyrus Hamlin, 1811-1900, who had come to Istanbul in 1839 and established a school for Armenian boys. Robert College developed well, and in 1971 merged with an American founded girls' school on a new campus, the old site now being occupied by the University of the Bosporus (Bogazici). See 'A College on the Bosporus', by M. P. and M. R. Stevens, *Saudi Aramco World*, March/April 1984, pp. 16-21.

don an apron and white cap to appear like a baker. C. and I played chess and I won. The captain got a turbot and some greens and fruit at Constantinople, also some small chairs.

FOUR

Ochikoff and Kherson
14-28 April

Reception at Ochikoff. Up-river to Kherson. Cricket v. SS Elswick Tower. Fat Mary the washerwoman. Inquisitive locals. Exploring the market. Ladies on board. Loading grain by hand. A country walk.

Ochikoff, now known in Ukranian as Ochikiv, is a small fishing port on a peninsula at the point where the Rivers Bug and Dnieper flow together into the Black Sea. The two rivers form an inland sea enclosed by a peninsula from the east on the south side Ochikoff stands at the mouth of this sea and thus controls access to both rivers and their ports.

Kherson, about twenty miles east, up the River Dnieper, is a port and an administrative and shipbuilding centre, with a population of 93,000 in 1914. It was founded by Prince Potemkin in 1778, on the authority of Catherine the Great.

14 APRIL   Friday. We arrived at the mouth of the River Bug before dinner and proceeded up it to Ochikoff. It has a very wide estuary and low banks on either side, and a strong fort at the entrance. At Ochikoff custom officials with soldiers and the Medical Officer came off for two hours. They had all hands on deck and took all names down. They sealed up large numbers of goods including my camera and queried at my silk neckerchief. Everybody's berth was inspected. Finally they gave the captain two sealed envelopes to deliver at our destination. The 'baker' was dressed in an apron and 1st Mate's night cap and created fun. The Russians of course wanted to know what he was and questioned him. At last with two pilots we proceeded and presently branched off up the Dnieper River. The banks are much narrower and the land only about one foot high. Higher banks appeared half a mile off, the others seeming to be the drained bed of the river. There are scattered houses and small hamlets about and gorgeous churches with white walls and bright green roofs. The houses are very poor looking, one-storey thatched. A few thin cows about and bare-legged women lounging about. There are lots of fishing boats, two waited at Ochikoff for two hours for a tow and then found we weren't going their way. We passed a couple of dredgers; our propeller churns up their yellow mud. About tea time we arrived at Kherson, a middle-sized town on a slope with scattered houses. More officers, etc., aboard and had another roll call and one soldier was left aboard as watchman. The captain alone was allowed ashore.

15 APRIL   Saturday. It was cold and bleak, clouded and a cutting wind so we sat over the fire and read during the morning. In the afternoon I started painting bulwarks to keep warm. After tea the captain of the *Elswick Tower* came aboard and beat the captain at chess. They then went ashore and I turned in about 10 o'clock.

16 APRIL   Sunday. After breakfast the captain went ashore and did not return till after tea. During the morning, by action of wind and tide, we were brought stern on to the quarter and stern of a St. Ives boat, the *Tregarthen*, bending the poop, rails and gunwale! I did a little amateur sailoring in the morning and afternoon hauling and slackening ropes and lowering fenders as we swung on and off. After tea our captain came aboard and the two talked about the damage for a long time; the captain of the *Elswick Tower* and our agent, a young dark featured Russian came with him and talked some time and went ashore again.[1]

17 APRIL   Monday. The captain brought some newspapers aboard, *Daily Mail* and an *Echo* and I spent the morning reading them. The captain, about 6 o'clock, remoored our ship and the Chief and Chips [*usual name for a ship's carpenter*] and some others went aboard the *Tregarthen* and helped repair the damage. The harbour master said it was his fault. After dinner I turned to and helped 1st and 2nd mates to paint upper bridge. After tea I read a little and listened to yarns from a meeting of officers in the 2nd Mates berth – 1st and 2nd mates, Chief and 2nd engineer and steward. The captain lunched and dined ashore.

18 APRIL   Tuesday. We are still lying in the stream but hope to be alongside tomorrow. In the morning and afternoon I have been painting upper bridge, aft, bulkhead and bulwarks. After

---

1. The damage was ultimately assessed at £663 13s 4d and was met by four parties in the proportions 60%, 6%, 3%, 31%. See note on p. 71 where the damage was much less and the proportions were equal. The parties would be Protection and Indemnity Clubs (PICs) to which Westolls belonged – 'protection' because they acted on behalf of their members to limit or reduce any claim or liability, 'indemnity' because they reimbursed the member for loss. In this case the names of the parties are illegible (even with ultra-violet light) in the Westolls record held by Tyne and Wear Archives Service, but the sums can be read and indicate the proportions noted. Most trading ships today are members of a UK-based P&I club.

tea I read Bret Harte,[2] lent by captain. After working hours the officers like to improve their berths. The 2nd mate lengthened the settee. The steward altered his wash stands and drawers and painted and then grained part of the walls. They then cleaned the paint off the brass ports and polished them, a job which I helped the 1st Mate at this evening. The old man has been unwell today and sat over the fire.

19 APRIL   Wednesday. Before breakfast we were moved alongside and now get a better view of the town. The captain at my request bought me some pictures of the town. After breakfast I wrote in my capacity of purser some letters for the captain, payment notes for some firemen and one signed by myself as purser saying 'Please pass these clothes for washing'. The washerwoman from Odessa, known as Fat Mary, came for the clothes and there was trouble about allowing them ashore. My permit and four gendarmes in about two hours settled the matter and finally the lady got away.

I read and watched the changing scenes from the deck. The men and women who load the boat passing about. They struck on the *Elswick Tower* and would not work if [grain] elevators were used. Finally all the women went away. Boat loads of women going to and from work sing peculiar minor songs in two or three parts. The seconds sing their parts higher than the tune which produces a peculiar effect. Russians are the only people who sing so.

The school boys play about the quay. They all wear uniforms and look like telegraph boys. Some have short blouse coats and trousers and look very well. Some have long bare frocked uniform coats and look very awkward like shrinking bandsmen. They play about like other boys, make see-saws of planks, and chuck wood in the river. They looked pale and thin, I thought, and smoked Russian cigarettes.

---

2. Francis Bret Harte (1836-1902), prolific American author and poet, inspired by Dickens, inspirer of Kipling. Appointed US Consul in Krefeld, Germany, in 1878 and Glasgow in 1880, settled in London in 1885.

Many carts come down to the river to water the horses which all have the wooden top yoke.

They are very curious about the ships. All sorts come aboard, mothers bring their children and inspect things and school girls come and talk to the men to learn English. Two talked a long time to a German fireman of ours [*the Crew List (p. 91) includes a fireman called C. Berbsten*]. After dinner I read again and then helped the mate in coiling up a new <u>lead line</u>. After that the captain sent me round to the *Elswick Tower* for a newspaper and after some trouble with the Russian sentry I was allowed to pass. I had a long talk with the captain of the *Elswick Tower*. The captain had a friend to tea and went out after and I spent a quiet evening.

20 APRIL Thursday. The captain squared the sentry and I was allowed into the town. I went a short way with the captain and then turned off by myself. The streets are wide but only the middle paved, with trees and a footpath at the sides and rows of trees between. I turned off at the fifth street into the main street. The shops were all small and most were closed as it was a Jewish holiday.[3] I walked round the town and broke my five rouble gold piece with cigarettes. I met the captain and he told me to go to the market, which I did. It is a large open space with strong sheds in which fish, rather poor fruit and other things were sold. Here one saw the natives best, the poor ragged serf, etc. Droshkies, low and small carriages abound and there are no trams. The only Russian I know is 'Nye ponomayoo' – 'don't understand', and the different letters prevent one reading at all. However the Russians themselves are so illiterate that all shops have signs with their goods painted on. In the market a man recognised my nationality and came up and said 'What is the

---

3. Passover or Pesach. At this time, one third of the population of Kherson were Jewish.

matter with you'. He knew very little English but said he had been to London. In the park I saw the statue of the Englishman.[4]

Although it was very hot there was an absence of shade, there being no leaves on the trees. I made my way back by one o'clock and after dinner sat on the poop, over which the awning had been spread, and read and mended C's chair with duck and a sail needle borrowed from the 2nd Mate. I had a long chat with him in the chart house where he was making pillows for the chronometer and he showed me how to make a *'turks head'*.

21 APRIL   Friday. This being Good Friday all hands had holiday and cross buns for breakfast. In the morning I went ashore again, visiting the Synagogue at the captain's recommendation to hear the fine singing.[5] About 10 o'clock I came out and sat in the shade and then bought some Peters Chocolate[6] in a very nice grocers shop. On the counter were counting beads [*an abacus*]. I visited the market and got C. some lemons and returned aboard. In the afternoon the captain had his friends aboard, six or seven of them, so we had tea with the Officers. After that we played the *Elswick Tower* at cricket, all accessories being made by them, and

4. Presumably the obelisk to John Howard, the philanthropist and pioneer of English prison reform, after whom the Howard League for Penal Reform was named. He became concerned about the infectious diseases rampant in prisons, and spent several months in Kherson studying their causes, and caring for sufferers, from one of whom he caught typhus and died on January 20, 1790, aged 63. A granite obelisk, with a bronze relief of his figure in profile (Pl. 22), was erected in 1806 at the wish of Alexander I and by public subscription, with the inscription in English and Latin: 'Whoever you were, here lies your friend'. There is also a statue of him in St. Paul's Cathedral. See DNB Vol. 28, pp. 390-394. Another Englishman, Samual Bentham, brother of Jeremy Bentham, was also closely connected with Kherson.
5. There are many Passover songs, most concerned with praising God's glory.
6. Daniel Peter, a candle maker in Vevey, Switzerland, converted his plant to making chocolate when oil became more widely used as lamp fuel. In 1975, after eight years experimenting in collaboration with a neighbour, Henri Nestle, he succeeded in making milk chocolate, being hailed as its inventor and winning a gold medal in Amsterdam in 1883. The business became owned by Nestle in 1951 and Cargill Inc. in 2002 but still trades as Peter's.

won by two innings to one. I scored 1 - 2 - 2 and caught some one each time which was fairly good as things went. I had a cold bath after and then a little practice on the 1st mate's Sandow exerciser [*patented 1892 and still flourishing*], and so to bed.

22 APRIL   Saturday. Some time after breakfast I went ashore. The sun was hot so I got two oranges and sat in the park eating them. I bought some Spirits of Nitre [*old-fashioned remedy for palpitations, flatulence, cold with fever, kidney medication, and in cases of dropsy*] for C. and then walked past the barracks and on board again. After dinner some ladies invited by the captain arrived, eleven of them so we cleared out on to the bridge deck and I chatted with the engineers. They went about five with the captain and we had tea with the officers. After tea we had two games of cricket.

23 APRIL   Easter Sunday. After breakfast the Chief Engineer produced an India rubber ball which he bought on Saturday, and Mr. Alderson proceeded to cover it with canvas. This took till 10.30 when we had a game of football with picked sides with *Elswick Tower*. Our side won, when we stopped exhausted with heat and exercise about 12 o'clock. I bathed myself out of a pail and felt very refreshed. After dinner (chicken) I read and talked. Presently the washerwoman, Fat Mary, arrived and we were very glad to see her as a rumour got afloat that she had vanished with our clothing. I spent a quiet evening reading 'The Mystery of a Hansom Cab' [*by Fergus Hume, 1859-1932*]. The captain sent on board 200 volumes of *Edinborough Reviews* and *Quarterly Reviews* a present from Mr. Karouana [*not otherwise identified*] so if all else fails, we can read them.

24 APRIL   Monday. This morning shows a great change in the weather, very cold with a strong wind up the river. I did not go ashore. During the morning and afternoon I sorted up the captain's *Quarterly Reviews* and *Edinborough Reviews*. There were ten short. After tea I kicked the football about a little to get warm and returned aboard to read, and to bed about 10.30.

25 APRIL Tuesday. Today is a little warmer as we have had some sun interspersed with showers. In the morning I went ashore for a walk and after dinner read and watched the loading of grain, forward with an elevator and aft with gangs. In the hold of the barge four women fill buckets which they hand to two others on a platform who hand them up to two others on the deck of the barge who empty them into a cask to be weighed by a man. He empties it into a sack which is lifted on to a man's back, and he carries it up gangways to the hatch and throws it down at a woman's feet. She empties it and folds it up.

After tea it rained again so we had no football and I stayed in the cabin and read. The 1st Mate came in and C. got on to his usual topic 'My young friend you have a lot to learn yet' and 'Young men think old men are fools but old men know young men are'.

26 APRIL Wednesday. Today has again been cold and showery. I did not go ashore but stayed on board and read, etc. After tea we had a short game of cricket without sides. The Russian labourers proved obstreperous, insisting on crowding round and throwing our ball about and shouting and laughing. As we did not want a riot we did not interfere much. The natives had a game to themselves, three of them putting their backs together and others somersaulting over them. In the morning we had a little amusement in seeing the captain fire a man off the poop [*not a known phrase*].

27 APRIL Thursday. We have been loading slowly all day and only one other ship remains here. The *Elswick Tower* sailed at six o'clock in the morning. I did nothing particular in the morning and after dinner cleaned my boots, shaved and walked to town to get some medicine for C. When seeking for the chemists I came across a man speaking English. When returning I met him again and during a short conversation I offered to get the address of a

London business directory. He keeps an English store, sells sewing machines and terracotta goods etc. Mr. N. A. Baltjansky, Chirson.[7]

After tea when it was dusk we looked about for the ducks but they were gone. I then had a game of whist with the Chief against the 3rd and steward and won and so ended the day.

28 APRIL   Friday. Our last day in Kherson. After breakfast I was soon out with the captain and went to the office of the agent Sidney Reed & Company and met Steingart. We arranged to meet and have a Russian dinner. I then left them and went a walk straight up to the market and out into the country. This is all gently up hill but out of the town it is level, a vast plain with sandy soil cut up in all directions with cart tracks and except for these covered with very thin grass. Large herds of horses and cattle feed about on this. Ahead is a cemetery enclosed with palings with gilt crosses and tombstones. The rough carts of the Russians, which are springless and formed of two unshaped tree trunks on wheels with lath sides, pass along in all directions.

On reaching the cemetery I turned off to the right towards some palings which enclosed some fields, and a village came in view as I passed by these. Each rough thatched house had a small field attached and each enclosed in its own palings and each lot set down in some proximity to each other but no order, making the main street a very wide crooked affair. There were two decent houses at the end of the village and a fine church. I pointed in the direction I thought Kherson would be and said Kherson and a boy said 'Da' and I soon found my way back. Finding it hot I bought two oranges and ate them in the park.

I then returned to the ship and washed and went to the office where we all three proceeded to the Hotel Odessa and had dinner. First some entrees, herring, radishes, etc. on various

---

7. Doubtless Mr. B's transliteration of the Russian name, here otherwise rendered as Kherson; the 'kh' letter (as also in 'Khrushchev') is pronounced as in the Scottish 'loch'.

dishes, and caviar with lemon. Then 'Bortsch', rich dark green soup in which floated for each a whole egg and meat. On this whipped cream is poured. Then lumps of meat on a skewer with rice. We had now enough and finished up with oranges. This heavy dinner made me sleep till tea time after which I played whist again and so to bed at 9.30.

FIVE

Nicolaieff and Odessa
29 April to 6 May

Tsardom detecting Russians on board. Football v. other British ships. A haircut for 7½d. Beekeepers show their hives. Jewish friends at home. Overnight by boat to Odessa. A fine hotel. Odessa's seaside resort. Dinner with the British shipping agent at home. Back in Nicolaieff, more socialising with British, Dutch, Russians. Local cavalry exercises. The Yacht Club. Shops shut for the Czarina's birthday.

Nicolaieff (the modern Ukrainian town of Mykolayiv) stands on the estuary of the River Bug, a few miles upstream from the Black Sea. In the late nineteenth century it had a population of 120,000. Like Kherson its access to the sea is controlled by Ochikoff. It also was founded by Prince Potemkin, in 1788 as a shipbuilding centre. It also became the chief grain port of southern Russia.

Odessa lies on the coast of the Black Sea itself, some 40 miles west of Ochikoff. It is a substantial city (late nineteenth century pop. 630,000), one of the most important commercial towns and ports on the Black Sea, and one of the grandest and best laid-out cities in Russia. It was founded by Catherine the Great in 1794, on the site of earlier Tatar and Greek settlements. It was a free port for most of the first half of the nineteenth century, and developed a very cosmopolitan ethos. At the end of the century more than a third of the population were Jewish, but they were the victims of some serious pogroms and the city became a major centre of support for Zionism. Two months after the author's visit Odessa became a centre of the Russian uprising of 1905, following a mutiny of sailors in the port – later made famous in Sergei Eisenstein's film Battleship Potemkin *(1925).*

29 APRIL Saturday. At 4.15 'all hands on deck' was the cry, and the inspector called over our names. I stood on the poop, rather cold, and watched Kherson recede as we left it to steam to Nicolaieff. After the last glimpse I turned in and slept again till 8 o'clock. After breakfast I checked the manifest B/L [*Bill of Lading*] and hold plan, and towards 12 o'clock Nicolaieff appeared in view. It has not such a fine appearance as Kherson as it lies on flat ground and at some distance from the river. However it looks more like a port with a good many ships and tall grain warehouses and elevators. A Westolls funnel attracts our attention and the boat turns out to be the *Lavinia Westoll* loading manganese ore. The *Elswick Tower* was surrounded with elevators and will get away tomorrow.

As the Russian Easter[1] now comes on we do not expect to start loading till Tuesday. We are boarded by officials and the captain shouts for the purser [*the author*] who has to make out a list of the crew with their nationalities, and the foreigners have to come aft to be interviewed.[2]

The officer whose work this is, is an old tall stout man with white whiskers and a smattering of all languages. With seamen who he suspects to be Russian he talks to them in their own language and then suddenly swears in Russian at them. If Russian this startles them and they are discovered.

1. The Orthodox Easter usually falls later than the Catholic Easter, depending on when Passover is. The Russian Easter falls one week after Passover.
2. Perhaps to apprehend Russians who had fled after the failed attempts at revolution in the Ukraine earlier that year.

After dinner I went ashore with C. who walks very badly and we took the horse tram to the town, half hour run. After C. made some purchases I saw him in the tram back and went a walk myself and returned about 5 o'clock with the notes of 25 R. changed.

After tea the *Lavinia Westoll's* men came along and challenged us to a game of football. We were soon there and played with some of the Derwin's [*not otherwise identified*] men and lost 1 - 3. After the game the 2nd Engineer [Philpot] recognised me, we having met at Browns [*not otherwise mentioned*], and we all went on board the *L.W.* and spent the rest of the evening in the Engineers Mess Room drinking lemonade and wine and playing whist, and returned on board about 10.30. The chief strained his leg in the match and some dissatisfaction was displayed about a fireman playing for the *L.W.* We also, with shut eyes, drew pigs on Philpot's book and drew squares in front of mirrors.

30 APRIL   Sunday. After breakfast I went up to town with Mr. Moore [*4th Engineer*] and Mr. Coulton [*3rd Engineer*], and we had a ten kopek ride and saw the town from the car. This is the Greek Church Easter Sunday or Paque, and all shops are closed and bells ringing. Not many people are about. As it was blazing hot we entered a Jewish restaurant clandestinely opened, and refreshed ourselves, and returned aboard the ship for dinner. Immediately after dinner, Coulton, Alderson [*2nd Mate*] and I went to a milk shop where the attraction is a lady called Olga. Some time after dinner Mr. Newton [*Mate*] and I returned to the town but reached it in pouring rain. We met our chief and 2nd and some *L.W.* men sheltering and walked along with them, passing a fine statue of an Admiral Grey [*not identified*] surrounded with old brass, cannon etc., to a Greek church which was however locked. We retraced our steps to another restaurant to shelter from the heavy rain and had lemonade. When we came out the rain had made rivers on each side of the drain-less streets and we had some difficulty in avoiding wet feet. We caught a car and returned for tea.

After tea I lounged as usual about the alley way and presently Mr. Newton and I went along to the *L.W.* where we found our chief and 2nd already installed in the Engineers Mess Room. Mr. Hodgson the Mate and Mr. Short the Chief and Mr. Philpot the 2nd Engineer [*all of the Lavinia Westoll*] were there and Mr. Short showed me his negatives. He is a great photographer and has had some of his published in the *Wire Co.* magazine, a snap of storks in a chimney and a wave breaking on the Bay and an article written and illustrated re the explosion aboard a vessel in the Black Sea. We then chatted and yarned on all subjects from church stories to conjuring and so passed the evening away.

1 MAY Monday. After breakfast I went to town to a barbers and had my hair cut at a cost of 7½d. I then walked up the main street and got into the park overlooking the river and returned to dinner after which I went around to the *L.W.* for the passenger, William Payne, and together we went to a beekeepers on the outskirts of the town. The owner is a friend of Mr. Short and W. P. had been already there. On arriving we found the old man asleep. His partner showed us round and opened the hives and we saw the queen and dead drones on the honey comb. He could not speak English however. Presently the bee keeper's daughter who is learning English came out and we had a jolly afternoon together. Her name is Jennie, age 18.

On arriving back at the ship I found the *L.W.* lady passengers leaving, and in the cabin some Jews, a pretty girl with large eyes and red lips called Helene, two older ladies and a young and an old man. Helene was the captain's great favourite and with an Italian conversation book he carried on conversation. The young man talked a lot to me and wrote my name in Russian and presently we went up to town. The young man and a lady left us and with Mr. and Mrs. Mickaelaeff and Helene we went to the park and sat listening to the band and were found by Captain Marshall and his lady passengers.

We presently went out, and leaving Captain Marshall and his ladies, visited the house of a Banker, Rosenberg. It was the first Russian house I had been in and was very nice: not much furniture but very good. Mrs. Rosenberg invited us to have some fruit and then we went to the Mickaelaeffs' house and had supper, mixed entrees and wine and jelly with Passover cake. Then manna bread, which tastes like plain sponge cake and is made in tall rounded cylinders, sometimes with fancy iced tops. We had tea out of a samovar. This is a tall tea urn with a fire inside and a place to hold the tea at the top, and making the tea is a complicated ceremony. The fireplaces attracted my attention. They are enclosed and of beautiful stone work and go up to the ceiling. All windows are double.

We saw the ladies to the Rosenberg house and returned in a rubber [*perhaps rubber-tyred*] <u>drosky</u> to our parakot [*?*]. I shoved a few things in my bag and made for the Odessa boat about 11.40. I got a nice bunk and soon lay down and the boat sailed at 12.30.

2 MAY Tuesday. I awoke and found myself in Odessa and going ashore hailed a drosky and despite bargaining my inexperience failed to get a drosky under 1 rouble [*about £5 in today's money – see p. 97*] so I drove to McNabb's (our agent) office and left my bag and went for a walk along the main street and visited a sort of hoppings[3] at the end. I then returned and had breakfast, coffee and 4 buns for 1/-. I then called at the office and saw Mr. Gallager whose name Captain N. had written down. As he was busy he sent me to Mr. Fleming who gave me a glass of wine and promised to meet me the next day.

I had lunch at the Europa Hotel to which I now took my bag and booked a room for 2½ R [*£12.50 today*] a day. The room was a beauty, first floor, high, narrow and long. In the middle a comfortable bed and wash basin and mirror. At the window end a table with three stuff chairs and couch and writing table, which I used to address some postcards. The Buffet Clerk spoke good English and directed me to the Little Fountain or in Russian Mali fountain to which I proceeded by tram.

---

3. A fair with roundabouts and sideshows, held on Newcastle Town Moor through the last week in June.

The Little Fountain is a seaside resort which is a great favourite in Odessa. It lies away from the city [*a few miles to the East*] and consists of a broad strip of broken up land ornamented with paths and trees and fancy temples and buildings, fronted by the sea and with a background of cliff. At one part is a large open air restaurant (pectopan) [*'p' is the Cyrillic alphabet transliteration of 'r' and 'c' of 's'*] where a band played. I had a coffee and sat listening a long time. The sun was warm but not hot and everything very pleasant. I returned about 8 o'clock and not feeling like dinner bought a cake at a stall. After a wash I strolled about the town and soon turned in feeling tired.

3 MAY Wednesday. I slept till 9.30 and went to have breakfast. I thought ham and eggs would be nice and had them in a wonderful dish, four eggs and bacon, very hot, and coffee, price 1 R. 20. I explored the town till 12.30 when I returned to the hotel to meet Fleming, and we had dinner together, turbot steak, red wine, coffee and a 'pudding'. We adjourned to the principal restaurant for more coffee and talk, and F. advised me to take a drosky to the Alexander Park[4] which overlooks the sea, is very pretty and a fashionable promenade. I explored it, visited a Greek church on its borders, and had an ice in the Park restaurant. The Alexandra column in the park is very fine.

I returned to the Bouvilon at 6 o'clock to meet Fleming and while waiting for him had coffee and watched all the fashionables parading. I met him at 7 o'clock and got my bag and we went to his house where I met his wife and we had supper together – sardines, duck and cucumber – after which he set me down to the boat, which left at 10 and landed me in Nicolaieff at 5 o'clock.

---

4. Immediately to the east of the city; the focus of the park is a monument to Alexander II, Tsar of Russia 1855-81, commemorating his visit to Odessa in 1875.

4 MAY Thursday. Back to the *Salient* I found the most important news to be that C. had fallen down the <u>Lazaretto</u> and was confined to bed. His eczema had commenced to scale very badly and the bruise on his side had brought on a congestion of lungs. He is to be put ashore at Constantinople. I went ashore with the captain about 10.30 and we bought some <u>separation cloths</u> which I brought down to the ship in a drosky. In the afternoon about 4 o'clock the Mouyiloff mother and daughter came aboard and we had tea together. Then went up to town and I left them to meet their clerk at the Barbe restaurant. I met another man who I had seen somewhere and presently met the clerk and we talked the evening through. A Dutchman living at Hull joined us late and as Captain Nicholson did not arrive and the cars had stopped, we arranged for a drosky together, it being rather dangerous after 10 o'clock. Captain Nicholson came up and we all went together to our boat, the Dutchman going to the Kherson boat.

5 MAY Friday. Captain Marshall and William Payne of the *Lavinia Westoll* came round early on and we went together for a walk. It was very dusty and windy. Presently we came to a park with the railing made of chains and the posts of old cannon stuck in the ground. To the right were some large barracks behind which on a large parade ground some cavalry men were exercising, riding at straw dummies with loose heads and cutting branches down etc., and this proving interesting we watched them some time, and returned aboard. After dinner I went to town and brought back some more separation cloths. I had an awkward time as they only spoke German and Russian and I was not sure of the price. At last, however, I got away with my load. After tea I took up a letter to Fischers office and returned immediately and met the 2nd Mate and 2nd and 3rd engineers and we adjourned to the '*Cardiff Castle*' where they had beer, and lemonade for me. A little girl, seven years old, played and sang

English songs very nicely and after that we had a game of Tip-it[5] and a few songs. We then adjourned to the Milk house, had a glass of milk, some tunes on a musical machine and a game of dominoes and returned to the ship.

6 MAY   Saturday. Our last day in Nicolaieff. It turned out to be one of the pleasantest. I was wondering what I should do and how to spend my last rouble when Mr. Short and Willie [*probably William Payne, the LW passenger*] came along. I joined them and we walked to the Custom House where S. was to pay a fine of 5 roubles for breaking the seal on his bicycle. We sat here about 1½ hours yarning and waiting for the man, who did not turn up, so we left and went aboard the *Lavinia Westoll*. I stayed to dinner with the engineers and then the 3rd, Mr. Allan, and Mr. Short and I went to town and Willie to Manasaus.

We had an 8 kopek ride to a very pretty wood on the river banks, where are the headquarters of the Yacht Club. It is very like an English club and we watched some Russians playing rounders, which they did in a very half-hearted fashion. We got some may, which had not the familiar English smell. Some of it smelt very much like heather honey.

We returned to town and had tea at a shop where splendid fancy cakes cost 3 kopeks each. We walked about the town and visited the post office, which was shut as this was the Czarina's birthday.[6]

We walked to Manasaus and found Willie there and bid goodbye to Jennie. Willie would not come with us. At a pub on our way down I bought some postcards and from a drosky man a *flint striker* as a curiosity. Again on to the *Lavinia Westoll*. Allan, Short, our Chief, Chapman, and Mr. Philpot played cribbage. They spread us a nice supper and we returned aboard.

5. An internationally popular indoor game for several players, in which each in turn tries to remove a small article such as a disc, without collapsing a large article balanced upon them.
6. Alexandra, wife of Tsar Nicholas II, was 30 on this day. In 1918 the couple and most of their family were executed by the Bolsheviks.

SIX

Back to home waters, calling at Constantinople
7-23 May

The Bosporus. Captain Donaldson the pilot. Santa Sofia. The Sultan's Tombs. The bazaar. The boy who wanted to get away. Crete and other islands. Boat drill. Sicily, Pantalaria, Cape Bon, Gibraltar close up. Cape St. Vincent's new lighthouse (but no girl). 'Coal fever', so I beat the captain at chess, and we divert to Dartmouth.

7 MAY Sunday. At 5 o'clock all hands on deck. We were counted and soon were away. We steamed away and after breakfast reached Ochikoff and got our papers in the morning. I got my camera out. We passed Odessa in the distance and started across the Black Sea. The captain and I had our first game of chess.

8 MAY Monday. A quiet day at sea, very pleasant after being ashore, sunny weather tempered with a cool breeze. We have some live stock, hens in a coop and yellow hammers and other small birds on deck, also some wasps and lady birds. After tea we had a game of chess.

9 MAY Tuesday. At 4.30 I got up and was soon on deck in an overcoat. The captain invited me on the bridge and I stood sheltered by the canvas watching the entrance to the Bosporus. The sun had not risen. The cliffs stretch straight ahead of us with a narrow break in them. On each side a piece is whitewashed and a lighthouse stands also on each side. As we approach we see castles on each side, all very ancient and in ruins. So we enter. The land on each side is rather wild, green and rock mixed. Soon we come to Crevac. Here our pilot came off, Captain Donaldson. He is well known on the Bosporus and always sings out as he comes 'full speed astern Captain Nicholson'. He was soon up on the bridge. The scenery changes and on each side are houses and palaces reaching up the sides of the land and with fine groves and woods of trees, the most brilliant of which was lilac in full blossom. We pass Swan's house and greet them and also the Sultan's new yacht[1] and Yildiz Kiosk[2] on the hill. We are now near Constantinople and presently enter the harbour. A little way back are two great old forts built by the Turks where they first crossed into Europe.[3]

As we entered the magnificent harbour the sun shone out full and strong on one of the finest sights in the world. The minarets gleamed in the sun. We steamed to our anchorage and dropped both anchors about 7.15. Old Donaldson said to the man at the wheel 'Put yer hellum amid ships and go to the devil'. Now ensued a busy time. I started to get into my shore clothes and then we had breakfast from some crisp little fish obtained from a boat to which we gave a tow. (At Crevac we received letters, five

1. Presumably the *Erthogroul*, built at Elswick Shipyard, Newcastle, in 1903. See Pl. 25.
2. Or Star Kiosk, a palace used by the Sultan at that time to house his administrative staff, set in a grand park overlooking the Bosporus on the European side.
3. In 1356, though Constantinople only fell to them in 1453. At the point where the Bosporus and the Black Sea meet, forts on either side of the straits were linked, at least until the time of the Crimean war, by a chain, which was used to delay enemy ships while they were fired upon from both sides.

20. "A magnificent two-funnelled yacht came out with the German Empress" (p.13). SMS Hohenzollern, the German Royal Yacht.

21. "The Queen was expected at 5 o'clock on the yacht" (p.25). In this photograph taken by the Queen on board the royal yacht in the Mediterranean in 1905, "little Olav" meets a group of officers, with Princess Victoria Alexandra (1868-1935) looking on. Published in Queen Alexandra's Christmas Gift Book - Photographs From My Camera, London 1908 (sold for charity).

22, 23. "In the park I saw the statue of the Englishman". (p.42; see footnote). 23, bas-relief, and 23, obelisk, in Kherson park, commemorating John Howard, 1726-70.

24 "I inspected it through the long glass… a fort which at one time must have been very powerful." (p.60). The castle at Tenedos.

25. "We… greet… the Sultan's new yacht" (p.56).
The Erthogroul, built at Elswick Shipyard, Newcastle, in 1903.

26. "I found my way back to San Sofia and photographed it". (p.59).

27. "We saw its full length and shape" (p. 64) – panorama of Gibraltar.

28. "We passed a beautiful barque" (p. 64).

29. A jackass barque.

30. "The Princess Heinrich, usually running from Genoa to the Riviera and now bound for Hamburg" (p.68).

31. "Further up the river are two old battleships… for cadet training." (p.67) This one is not HMS Britannia.

32. A regatta or race, probably off the English south coast.

33. "I was soon dressed and we were rowed ashore." (p.69)
Waterfront in Holland, possibly where they landed when moored in the Rhine Haven.

34. Scheveningen is "…a seaside resort, with broad clean sands, large hotels and a pleasure pier." (p.72)

35. "…children with wooden clogs" (p.71)

36. "…women with Dutch headdress" (p.71)

37. "I presently found the Palace" (p.72)
– possibly the Palace in the Wood

38. "a curious custom: instead of our stiff 'Keep off the Grass'" (p.75)

39. "The chief and he were off to meet the train from the Hook" (p.69). GER's SS Amsterdam.

40. "An imposing Gothic church with an immensely high steeple, beautifully decorated." (p.73).

41. "We… steamed up the Tyne and reached Dunston" (p.76).
SS Salient alongside Dunston staithes, loading with coal for the next voyage.

to me). I then finished dressing, put 40 films in the camera and then helped C. to dress and pack his box. I copied a letter for the captain and we set off ashore in a steam launch. C's trunk was lowered and with difficulty he got into the boat. He was quiet but pleased to be ashore.

We reached the quay and C's box was examined. I proceeded to Swan's office with my guide, a Greek who appeared from somewhere. Old Mr. Swan kindly gave me a few tips and restrained the man and we [*his companion was apparently his guide*] set out with one sovereign. This we changed at a money changers and I bought some cigarettes and received back dollars ¾ on majiavestas [?] piastres @? & paras (40 to a piastre). We walked across the Galata Bridge, a wooden floating affair with a great deal of traffic and into the quarter of Stamboul and got into a carriage to go to the great mosque Santa Sofia.

Entering the gates and crossing the yard we passed into the entrance hall and received slippers. The entrance fee was one dollar. Passing under a heavy curtain and along a wide passage we turned into the church, a great hall, circular and with an enormous dome and the greatest church in the world. Far away up the dome pigeons cooed and flew about. The walls and dome are all inlaid with pure gold and present a wonderful appearance. The guide pointed out where the Turks defaced the Christian signs and substituted their own; some crosses etc. still remain. The floors are all covered with carpet and matting. On the walls are large boards bearing Koran texts. On one wall is a hand mark connected with some mysterious legend which I could not quite understand, something about the Sultan riding in on a horse and a lot of Greek girls. At one corner is a fountain consisting of a large rounded block of stones and with taps. The supply is a mystery. A tunnel runs below in which a man once went and was never seen again.

We went out by an enormous door of iron hard wood the same age as the church, 700 years. When the sultan first went out the doors stuck open and have never since shut. The Greeks on the Pera side have a copy of the Santa Sofia without the rich work.

Outside nearby is an Egyptian column, one of three of which Cleopatra's Needle is one.[4] Here also is a magnificent fountain, like a small round temple, presented by the Kaiser three or four years ago. This part has many trees and is very pretty. From here we went to the Sultans' Tombs where three Sultans are buried, the chief being Makmoud. The guide pointed out four clocks given by Queen Victoria. In the Sultan's chamber are four or five coffins. The men have a fez on one end and Makmoud an insignia of glittering brilliante and diamonds.

On a cloth covered stool near these coffins rests, wrapped up in a green cloth, the Koran – the original volume, one similar being at Mecca. It is written on parchment and beautifully illuminated in the style of old English Bibles. Nearby is a large and ancient box covered with pearl, and locked. A messenger from the Sultan comes every morning and inspects the Koran and coffins and puts a signed paper in this box. On the wall hangs a plan of the Temple of Mecca. In another room are the tombs of Makmoud's wives. Outside in a garden are those of some of his pashas ['*provincial governor or other high official of the Ottoman empire*'].

From here we proceeded to the bazaar, the entry being by a mosque. The bazaar consists of narrow rounded corridors built in all directions; to go through all would take days and days. All sorts of things are sold in different sections. We entered by the jewellers; many beautiful ornaments and adornments are for sale. We passed where carpets are sold; one plain looking square the guide said was worth £40. We entered one shop and I made my purchase, a cushion cover 3/-, getting 2 piastres change out of a dollar.

We crossed over the bridge again into Galata and went up a tunnel railway into the modern and fashionable town, Pera. Here are English and French shops. In one I bought some postcards and examined my camera. We walked along the main street and

---

4. Cleopatra's Needle is one of a trio of Egyptian obelisks, of which the other two had by 1905 already gone to Paris and New York.

then returned and entered a Greek restaurant and had for dinner some fish, beef steak, rice and tomato and Turkish coffee. The Turkish coffee is black, very finely ground, and feels smooth to the taste like chocolate, and is sweetened. After dinner I paid my guide two dollars and we returned over the Galata Bridge into Stamboul. I dismissed my guide and strolled away alone through the old streets. I got into all sorts of odd streets and in one, looking into a yard, I saw a group of men in very little clothing. They presently snatched up a small pump on trestles and started off at a run. I then understood them to be the Fire Brigade. I found my way back to Santa Sofia and photographed it.

As my time was getting short now I strolled back and had a cup of coffee in a restaurant, 1d. Many were the strange sights to be seen. Turks, Greeks, Arabs, Armenians, Jews and other nationalities. The Greeks play backgammon very much. The Turks sit smoking their hubble-bubbles or chibouks ['*a Turkish tobacco pipe with an extremely long stem*']. I bought some oranges and a cigarette holder.

I reached Swan's office prompt at four o'clock but the captain did not turn up till five. A lady speaking French seems very anxious to get her son off as apprentice on our boat, the difficulty being about his passport. The whole story proved a curious one. The boy had money left him. The woman married a second husband and wanted the boy's money. Swans wanted the boy away and so did his mother. The boy stuck where he was and bribed the clerk to help him, which they did by forgetting to have his passport visa-ed. Captain Nicholson said he would take him but really would rather not. In the end they went to the Custom House, the boy was refused and we came away. He had to go to prison for attempting to leave the country.

We reached the *Salient* but as we got on board a valve or cock near the donkey boiler blew off, emitting clouds of steam, and this delayed us another two hours. The engines had not run satisfactorily today. When we entered the Bosporus she would not reverse as there was no vacuum from the condenser [*which condenses steam discharged after use in the cylinders*]. We had to take a brass tube ashore to be duplicated. As we started, our anchor fouled on a broken wreck and we only got clear by going full speed ahead and nearly tearing the <u>windlass</u> from the bows. This is quite a chapter of accidents.

Presently at eight o'clock we steamed away leaving the lights of Constantinople behind and as we emerged into the Sea of Marmora I turned in.

10 MAY Wednesday. Immediately after breakfast we passed the town of Gallipoli, from which port olives and fruit are exported. It is a very old and quaint Turkish town. We are now in the Dardanelles with land on each side. We passed Shenac and hoisted our flag to salute the Sultan's fort. We passed close to the opposite shore and as the captain had invited me on to the Upper Bridge I inspected it through the glass. There was a fort evidently of great antiquity.. The next place of interest is Tenedos Island [*now the Turkish island of Bozcaada, off the Turkish coast near Troy.*] I inspected it through the long glass [*the usual mariners' term for telescope*]. It is a straggling town of old houses planted indiscriminately and with a fort which at one time must have been very powerful (*see Pl. xx*).

From Tenedos we steamed away through the Grecian Archipelago with islands on all sides. The carpenter has been making a garden seat for the poop. We almost got one from the *L.W.* but Captain M. at the last minute repented. At dinner time it was finished and after dinner I painted. As the sun came out very clear and strong it proved a very warm job. After tea we played chess and I won my first game partly because the Captain tried to read a newspaper at the same time. We had a second game in which I was worsted. After this I had a hot bath out of a pail and soon after went to bed.

11 MAY Thursday. This morning I joined the captain on the bridge. He pointed out Crete in the far distance. At the moment it is agitating for junction to Greece [*which it secured in 1913*]. We passed Point Malla, which the Greeks thought to be the end of the world, and just before tea time the old man's corner opposite Cerigo Island [*better known as Cythera, in classical times*

131

[sketch of ship] 1st Tuesday May 1905

From Tenedos we steamed away thro the Grecian archepeligo. with Islands on all sides. The Carpenter has been making a garden seat for the poop. We almost got one from this. W but Capt M. at the last minute repented. At dinner time it was finished and after dinner I painted. as the Sun came out very clear & strong It proved a very warm job. after tea we played chess & I won my first game partly because the Captain tried to read a newspaper at the same time. We had a second game in which I was worsted. After this I had a hot bath out of a pail & soon after went up to bed.

Thursday, May 11th

Facsimile of a page from the original diary

the island of Aphrodite, the Goddess of love]. He has a chapel and a house, the chapel appearing first. The captain steered very close for my benefit. When opposite we gave a tootle on the whistle and he answered by ringing the bells in his chapel. He never appeared but we could see his donkey grazing. After tea the captain won at chess, he playing minus one bishop. Later we sighted C. Matapan, falsely styled the most southerly point of Europe, really W. Europe.[5]

12 MAY   Friday. We are having beautiful weather. Today rather cloudy but calm sea with a slight swell. I amused myself during the morning with reading this diary through. After dinner I did a job for the captain in the Chart House, filling in the details of the parcels of grains in our various holds on to a plan. After that I read and talked till tea time. After tea we had our game of chess, I won, the captain playing minus one Bishop. After the game I went forward and chatted with the 1st and 3rd engineers in the alleyway where we were presently found by the captain.

13 MAY   Saturday. I started a new job this morning, writing the names on the charts [*a matter of bringing up to date with changes observed*]. I also painted two 2's on the hatches, which had been painted out. Every Saturday we have rice for dinner. About three o'clock the chief started to teach me cribbage and we played till four o'clock when boat drill started [*see pl. 11*] The crew is divided for the two lifeboats, the captain taking the starboard one and the Mate the port one. I was for the port one. All hands then hoist the boat up and swing it out and swing it in again. Sicily was sighted this morning and after dinner we were close to it. Through the long glass it appears a beautiful country, well wooded and watered. The peculiar rigged fishing boats of the Sicilians are seen about in twos. Playing without his bishop the captain won a hard fought game of chess.

---

5. In fact, of mainland E. Europe. Cape Matapan or Tainaro is the most southerly point of mainland Greece, but the southern tip of Spain is slightly farther south.

14 MAY Sunday. At 8 o'clock we passed the Isle of Pantalaria [*or Pantellaria, a small volcanic island, part of Italy, mid-way between Sicily and Tunis*], remarkable for having a lake thousands of feet above sea level. It is a mountainous island. Sunday on board ship is very quiet, very little doing and no one to watch working. At dinner time we sighted Cape Bon on the African Coast and after that Islands of Tembra and Tembretta. Although right on the road to the Black Sea, India and Australia, we saw very few ships. After dinner, however, we sighted a few: an oil tanker of 11,000 tons, two Indian boats and a warship. After tea we played chess and after that the captain played Patience. When he had done I played till 10 o'clock and turned in. During the day we passed a spot where the captain said lately an island 800? feet high sprang up on a single night.

15 MAY Monday. Rather a dull day. There was a heavy swell causing a little water to come aboard and the ship to roll. In the afternoon I played cribbage, also after tea chess.

16 MAY Tuesday. The swell had entirely subsided when I got up and throughout the day it has been a peerless Mediterranean day, bright sun but not too warm. Everything is being painted and in the morning I did some varnishing on the poop. After a quiet afternoon of reading and talking I played chess with the captain in which I was quickly beaten. We then paced the poop and watched the sunset. Twilight quickly went and night came on with a beautiful moon nearly full. After this we played chess again, the Captain minus his Bishop and I won. Then we had a heated argument about politics, the captain like most sailors being a Conservative,[6] until he retired to the chart room at 10.15.

---

6. The author's father was a leading Sunderland Liberal. The following year, 1906, the Liberals won a general election by a landslide.

17 MAY Wednesday. This morning we reached the Spanish Coast and passed Cape de Gutto. Except for being dull in the morning it has been very fine.

18 MAY Thursday. Soon after breakfast we sighted Gibraltar ahead. The top covered with mist. We reached it about 10 o'clock. As we got up to it the mist slightly lifted and we saw its full length and shape, like a lion resting with its head on its paws and tail sticking out to sea [*Pl. 27*]. This is the view from the Mediterranean side. At one part on the face of the rock is an immense cement work into which runs a railway. This side is not so well fortified as the other, being much steeper. On the top is the signalling station, a triangular network of steel. It is decorated with bunting as this is evidently some special event. There is also an old tower, a flagstaff and a wire arrangement for hauling things up. From the rock to the mainland is very flat and the Spanish town is on one side, in front of it being the neutral ground. The ships in the harbour show up.

The captain kindly took us very close in and I saw everything to perfection. The extreme point is lower, representing the tail. A large yellow building is the Governor's (Sir G. White's)[7] house and there is also the lighthouse and wireless telegraph standard [*a mast*]. Going past we see the Atlantic side, which runs up to a razor edge at the top. There are bushes right up and no guns to be seen. Warships are seen in the harbour and outside lie the *coalhulks* which will be broken up when the harbour is finished [*building of new dockyards had been started in 1894*].

One *hulk* was once the largest wooden sailing ship in the world. On the African side Apes' Hill is prominent. A smart torpedo destroyer cruised about and we passed a beautiful barque among other ships. We finally turned the corner and about 12.30 passed C. Europa. After this I painted some lifebuoys and we

---

7. General Sir George Stuart White, 1835-1912, defender of Ladysmith in the Boer war (1899-2001), then Governor of Gibraltar, where he was appointed Field-Marshal on a visit by Edward VII in 1903.

passed Trafalgar bay about 3 o'clock. After chess I chatted with the Chief then read and turned in about 10.

19 MAY   Friday. About 9 o'clock we passed Cape Sagres where is a signalling station and later Cape St. Vincent[8] where is a lighthouse on the top of the high and precipitous cliffs. We passed very close and the captain blew the whistle in order, as he afterwards explained, to attract attention of a girl who used to wave a table cloth. However, she did not appear. There were a large number of masons there building the new lighthouse. In the afternoon we passed a school of five porpoises who swam very close to the ship. We also caught up to the *Derwent* [*unidentified*] which was in Nicolaieff with us (I met both the captain and the chief). We dipped our ensign to her. Then we met the *Gerent* of Westolls going south and hoisted our house flag. About 8 o'clock we passed Cape Roca.

20 MAY   Saturday. All day again it has been very warm. I played cribbage with the chief. After dinner a whale was sighted blowing in the distance but I did not catch sight of it. Early this morning the smoke of the *Derwent* was visible on the horizon. Four o'clock was boat drill at which I hauled ropes and made myself useful. After tea I won at chess, the captain playing without his Bishop. I finished reading Bleak House.[9]

21 MAY   Sunday. We entered the Bay of Biscay at one o'clock and when I got up the weather had already changed and was dull and gloomy and slightly cold. Throughout the day this has got worse, the wind ahead rising and the swell increasing so that we shipped some water. The captain and chief begin to worry about our coal supply, which was only calculated to just reach

8. Site of a British naval victory over a Spanish fleet in 1797. The windswept rocky headland rises 60m/200ft above the sea and the lighthouse, commissioned in 1846, is 24m/80ft high, its light visible from 35km/22mi.
9. By Charles Dickens, 1853; became a major BBC television series in 2005.

Rotterdam. This makes the captain gloomy and preoccupied and perhaps enables me to win our games of chess. It is a raw night and chilly sitting still so I turned in early and read in bed.

22 MAY Monday. Today the weather is worse, head wind and heavy seas and we struggle on through this all day [*see p.95, note 4*]. The captain and chief are very quiet and worry about the coal or as sailors say have 'coal fever'.

In the morning a steamer was seen ahead on the port bow, we drew nearer and passed under her stern, the '*Roma* of Whitby' and all day we steamed fairly close together. A Westolls boat, the *William Middleton*, passed us. It was very cold all day and when we played chess I fairly shivered and went to bed early and finished the Deemster by Hall-Caine.[10] The seagulls enjoy this weather and fly round the ship giving discordant shrieks.

23 MAY Tuesday. This morning the sea is very much calmer and we proceed very much faster. The sun broke away from the clouds and shone all day. The N.E. wind was very cold, however. The *Roma* had in the morning fallen behind and we went our different ways. After passing Ushant we turned off to coal at Dartmouth in Devonshire. Ushant is a very dangerous point and is where the *Drummond Castle* was lost.[11] It is something like Marsden [*on the County Durham coast*], isolated rocks sticking up. The lighthouse is one of the most powerful in the world, it throws the light 60 miles.

---

10. A successful first novel published in 1887, set in the Isle of Man. Deemsters are Manx judges.
11. She went aground off Ushant in June 1896 with the loss of 245 lives.

SEVEN

Dartmouth, Rotterdam, and Tyne
24 May to 8 June

Longshoremen. Battleships' target practice. The Hook and Rotterdam. Meeting visitors from home. The zoo. The Hague, Scheveningen and the Palace in the Wood. Antwerp via Roosendaal by train, its zoo and museum. On to Brussels. Down to the Hook and across to Flamborough Head. Arriving at Dunston. Reunited with family.

24 MAY   Wednesday. Early this morning we arrived in Dartmouth and when I got up and went into the cabin I found the Customs Officers inspecting. I then went on deck and found two hulks coaling us. We received 50 tons of coal by 9.30. Dartmouth is a lovely little spot and is a great yachting centre. Further up the river are two old battleships, the *Britannia* and another, for cadet training. On the top of a hill at one side is a large new building soon to be used instead of them. In front of us lies the town, straggling and quaint, and above, hills covered with trees. The harbour is almost land-locked.

At seven we had breakfast and then the captain and I proceeded ashore. The captain soon transacted some business at the Company office and we then inspected the town, which is very picturesque, and bought postcards, newspapers etc. The captain also bought a pair of boots and a fountain pen. There is a very pretty town square with trees and a bandstand. When we got on shore we heard a boat blowing for a pilot. It was the *Princess Heinrich*,[1] usually running from Genoa to the Riviera and now bound for Hamburg. We saw it at Gibraltar steaming after us but she must have felt the rough weather in the Bay for her paint work was washed off. We were told she burns 40 tons of coal per hour when going 19 knots an hour.

We met several examples of a type the captain told me about — 'longshoremen' in jerseys and fairly stout. They kept coming and saying 'Nice day for a sail' or 'Begging your pardon but where might you be bound for?'. They are said to say, if asked whether they are sailors, 'My hair's rope yarn and my blood pure Amsterdam tar'.

We got under way about 10 o'clock. The entrance is very beautiful, narrow and slightly winding with steep wooded cliffs on each side. Fine villas nestle among the trees with little summerhouses and boat landings and water falls. On one side is an old church and graveyard. The sea outside is a popular waterway and steamers, sailing ships, fishing fleets and pleasure yachts are on all sides.

As we neared Portland Bill after dinner two battleships appeared on the horizon and we hoisted our ensign. Each towed a target and as she approached they started firing at them. They passed fairly close and the spray of the shots around the targets could be plainly seen. Smokeless powder was used and the only other sign of firing was the reverberating boom of the guns. As we passed Portland Bill they proceeded in. On Portland Bill is a lighthouse and a larger new one being built. There is also a naval signalling station and a large building on the right we took for the prisons. After this we came to the Sands [*the Goodwins are farther east, however; see note on p. 5*] and lightship and as twilight fades away, to the St. Catherine's Point lighthouse, Isle of Wight [*see p. 5 and pl. 5*].

---

1. See p. 25 above. A paddle-driven passenger ship, built 1902. See pl. 30.

25 MAY   Thursday. Morning found us passing Dover about seven o'clock and we sight the lightship in the afternoon and after that our way lay between the sands and shoals. After tea we passed the Maas lightship. About 6 o'clock we got a pilot and started away at full speed for the Hook to catch the tide. I had a bath and shave and just finished as we entered. On our left we passed the Harwich passenger boat and for the next 3½ hours steamed up to Rotterdam, passing innumerable works and ships. The Agent's boat brought us the letters and we heard of several of Westolls boats being in the river. We moored about 12 o'clock and I turned in half an hour later.

26 MAY   Friday. At 4.30 I was aroused with a start by the captain asking if I did not want to go ashore. The chief and he were off to meet the train from the Hook.[2] I was soon dressed and we were rowed ashore. From here we took a ferry-boat and thus reached the Beurs (bourse) Station with half an hour to spare. The station time is English, 20 minutes before Dutch time [*see note on p. 13*]. The chief's and mates' wives arrived by that train and the chief took them off in a carriage. We then went to the Maas station and then hurriedly to the central to meet the next. In the next after that Mrs. Nicholson and a little boy called Neville arrived at 8 o'clock and we drove in a cab to the ferry and soon on board to breakfast.

   We are lying in the Rhine Haven which is full of shipping and great barges taking the cargo from boats. Between us and the next harbour, the Maas Haven, is a stately row of trees, and trees appear all over the docks. By the time breakfast was over the decks were full of men arranging for the *cargo 'jumping'*. About eleven I got a boat and went ashore and found the ferry and after some wandering found myself near the Zoo. I went in, paid 40 cents and 10 for the plan and went round. Everything was very

---

2. The Harwich-Hook ferry was run at this time by the Great Eastern Railway. Ships in service on it included the Amsterdam, Berlin, Vienna, Chelmsford, and Cambridge (see pl. 39), the first three around 1750 <u>GRT</u>, the other two smaller.

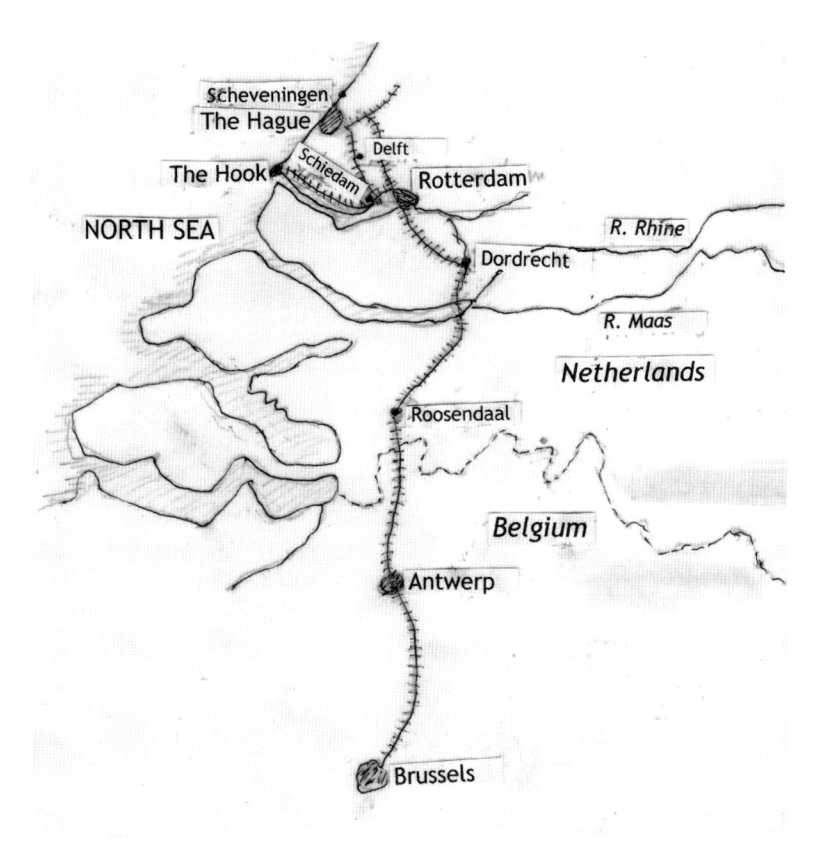

Visits from Rotterdam

interesting and the whole laid out a beautiful way. I just got round by 2.30 when the larger animals are fed and after seeing this went away, got to the High Street and had some dinner and set away to find the boat. This was a difficult job, the numerous canals making it impossible to remember the way. I arrived, however, a little after five and had tea and did not go ashore again, spending the time till 8 o'clock chatting with the officers and amusing the boy. Being tired I turned in about 9 o'clock.

27 MAY   Saturday. After breakfast the captain, 1st mate, 1st apprentice and 4th engineer went ashore to make a declaration about us running down a barge on entering.[3] I went with them and left them at the office and went along to the Maas Station, making calls to change some money, to buy stamps and a guide book and to have a glass of milk. At the Maas station I got into a passenger boat which at 11.30 took me up the river. The scenery was typical Dutch, windmills, straight avenues of trees, barges of all sorts. About one o'clock I arrived at Dordrecht [*25kms southeast of Rotterdam*] which is a quaint old town with narrow and old streets, children with wooden clogs, women with Dutch headdress and dogs in carts. I had dinner in a nice restaurant and returned by the 3 o'clock boat and got aboard in time for tea. Captain Stephenson has been aboard since we arrived and we had a pleasant time. After tea I chatted with the 3rd and 2nd mates.

28 MAY   Sunday. About 11 o'clock I took a boat to the shore and proceeded to the central station and booked a return ticket to The Hague. A train soon left, about 11 o'clock, and half an hour later I was there, the distance being 12 miles. On getting into the town I was at a loss what to do, for I had the vaguest idea of the place. I walked into the town and at a stationers bought a guide and got some information. Over a cup of coffee I

---

3. The 'Damage to lighter at Rotterdam' was assessed at £1 5s 0d and was met in equal parts (give or take 1d.) by four parties – Sunderland, North of England, UK, and one other. See note on p.39.

read the guide and then took the electric tram to Scheveningen, three miles away, for 12½ cents. Steam, horse and electric[4] trams run and it is a splendid and lively run – motors, carriages, bicycles and foot passengers throng the road and make the scene lively. We pass by lovely woods in which is the 'Palace in the Wood'[5] and by cool canals, and arrive at Scheveningen, a seaside resort, with broad clean sands, large hotels and a pleasure pier. I walked about, then had dinner and after 2.30 went on the pier, 10 cents. A band performance started then, to which I listened for an hour, and then took the tram back.

I got out before it reached The Hague and entered the woods. In the broad carriage drives and cool walks thousand of people were enjoying the air. There are hundreds of fine large trees and beautiful grassy slopes. Ornamental canals run through and it is a very fine place. I reached a café where a band played but I passed on and soon came out of the other side of the wood. Here I got fresh directions and presently found the Palace which is not very impressive looking, though well situated. I now retraced my steps and had a look round the town and saw a fine arcade. I caught a train about seven o'clock and was back on board by eight o'clock, very tired. The Dutch peasant girls in their best national costumes were very interesting but shy about being photographed. The train passed Delft, a quaint old town where the ware is made, and Schiedam, noted for gin.

29 MAY   Monday. Today has been scorchingly hot. I went ashore and walked about the streets and visited the Baymans Museum, a picture gallery of Dutch and Flemish artists. After this I went to the park and so on board for tea time. After tea I lounged about and went to bed at 10 o'clock.

4. Electric trams had been pioneered in the early 1880s in the USA, Canada, Russia and Germany.
5. The royal palace, home of the kings of Holland, built initially at the end of the sixteenth century, and greatly extended in the early nineteenth century.

30 MAY Tuesday. After some thinking over in the morning I decided to go Antwerp, so as soon as I could get a boat, which is not always immediately, I got a rope rigged to slide down on to the lighter. I proceeded ashore with sufficient things packed in a small bag including the camera. At 11.20, Greenwich Time [*see p. 69 and note on p. 13*], the train started. The journey was interesting, the scenery being typical. For much of the way we ran along the banks of canals and once passed a sort of estuary where fishing boats and barges were sailing about. At Roosendaal we arrived at the Belgian frontier and had to change trains, waiting half an hour, during which time I had some lemonade and a wash and bought two postcards and was rushed with a Swiss ½ franc. Our Belgian train (the engine with a square funnel) soon brought us to Antwerp and a man took my bag and directed me to the Queens Hotel. This was a good long way, it is on the quayside, Captain Nicholson recommended it to me.

It was now after 3 o'clock. The proprietress gave me a room and a small plan of the town and I left to see the cathedral[6] which was close by. It is an imposing Gothic church with an immensely high steeple, beautifully decorated. One franc admits one inside after 2 o'clock when the pictures are unveiled. There are especially two triptychs of Rubens, representing the Ascension and descent from the Cross. They are large, world famous and beautiful. The church inside was very lofty and decorated and of late perpendicular construction [*Gothic architecture had been a leisure interest of the writer when at school*] had much fine carving and stained glass.

After leaving here I, as usual in new towns, looked round for an English guide book and soon found one. I then went and had an agonising shave and walked on and passed St. Jacques church, also old, and on to the park which is very pretty. From here I proceeded to the Zoo, which is good but suffered in comparison

---

6. The Cathedral of our Lady was begun in 1352 and became a cathedral in 1559. It is described as 'a masterpiece of lace work in stone' and 'one of the finest gothic buildings in Europe'. See pl. 40.

with that of Rotterdam. They had some fine seals, sea lions and elephants, however. Also the animal houses were built in diverse architecture, the Lion House being Moorish or Assyrian and the Elephant House, Egyptian, with sloping entrances and hieroglyphics on the walls. I now went back to the hotel and had a good dinner a la table d'hote and sallied out to find a circus I had seen advertised. However I got to the wrong place, a Comedie Francaise where a comedy was enacted. However I understood a fair amount of the sense and enjoyed it.

31 MAY Wednesday. I awoke late (9.30) and after breakfast went out into the town to the museum[7] which is the great place of Antwerp. It is a magnificent building with a columned entrance. I first examined the statuary on the ground floor left and then on the ground floor right, prints of all P. P. Rubens pictures, a complete collection numbering some hundreds. They were very interesting and took a long time to examine. From these I went to the first floor where are the oil paintings, most of Flemish schools including very good ones of Rubens, Van Dyck, etc. It has been dull weather all day so I did not photograph anything but walked about. There are some old and quaint buildings in Antwerp especially round the cathedral. Also on the quay an old castle, the Stein. A Belgian battleship lay alongside still in commission but very out of date. After dinner I found the real Hippodrome and so passed the evening.

1 JUNE Thursday. At 10.20 am I had settled my bill, left the Queens Hotel and was in the train for Brussels. On arriving at the station du Nord I took a tram to the Midi Station and trammed back to the Nord and commenced my tour as per guide book. This led me to the principal places and streets, and I then saw the Bourse, the town hall and guild hall, the Mannikin

---

7. The Royal Museum of Fine Arts, built in the style of a Neoclassical temple during the late 1880s.

statue, the Park, Art Gallery with some fine pictures especially Rubens, the Palace of Justice,[8] which is a magnificent modern building on the hill top, the Porte de Hal. a museum of old armour and artillery large and small, and the Bois de Cambre, one of the finest of parks with grassy glades and tall trees. I walked as far as the lake and returned. They have a curious custom: instead of our stiff 'Keep off the Grass' something like this in French 'The trees give us their share and with the flowers and grass gratify our senses, therefore to destroy them is to rob ourselves of pleasure'.[9] I now found myself with very little time it being 4 o'clock so I got trams to the Midi Station, had a little dinner, caught the 4.53 Paris Express to Rotterdam via Antwerp, and was on board again by 9 o'clock. It is a holiday today, Ascension Day, so everywhere is gay and the weather has been very sunny. In Brussels I saw several girls dressed in white with long veils like brides.

2 JUNE Friday. I found the *'Virent'*, Captain Alexander, moored next to us. This was the last day in port. I went ashore about 10 o'clock and looked round the town again and found the arcade, a place I had not seen before. I also explored the park which is very beautiful, had lunch, made some purchases and came aboard for tea. After tea Captain Stephenson left us to go home by the Harwich boat. We partly expected to sail today but shall not do so until tomorrow.

8. Said to be the biggest nineteenth century building in the world – 105 m high and covering a total surface of 24.000 square metres. It still functions as the supreme court of law for Belgium.
9. The inscription still exists, mounted above eye level on an ornamental post and frame, with the text in French and Flemish, but rusted over and almost illegible. The words can be made out: 'Les arbres nous donne ... / ... avec les plantes ... et la beaute... / Abimer les arbres et les plantes / c'est se faire du tort a soi-meme'. See pl. 38.

3 JUNE Saturday. After breakfast we had all cargo out and about quarter to ten got under way and by mid-day were out of the Hook. This voyage is very interesting: many ships passed and quaint towns, Delft, Schiedam etc. During the afternoon it got misty but cleared away before night, the sea being very calm with a southerly wind. I spent the evening getting things together and preparing for the end of my voyage.

4 JUNE Sunday. Soon after breakfast we sighted Flamborough Head and steamed up the English coast. During the morning I employed myself in helping the captain in calculating the pay due to sailors [*see the Crew List (p. 91)*].

About 2.30 we arrived and a tug came out and first made us think we had to go Sunderland. It was not so, however, but we had to wait till the tide ebbed to go straight up to Dunston. At 3.30 we started and steamed up the Tyne and reached Dunston 5.30. The captain and family and chief and his wife and self, after mooring, sailed down again to Tyne dock in the tug boat and caught the train home. At Sunderland station I found father waiting for me and we all went home together, where I found mother, Willie and Jack all glad to see me and hear my news and so to bed at 10.30.

5 JUNE Monday. By the 9 o'clock train I went over to South Shields meeting Mr. Chapman [*not identified*] in the train. We walked about South Shields meeting Mr. Newton and others of the *Salient* at the Mill Dam [*see p. 1, note*]. About 10.40 Captain Nicholson arrived and we entered the Merchant Marine Office and paid off. I assisted Captain Nicholson to count money and check pay notes and then received my own discharge note which I shall keep. The officers signed on again and then, it being after 12 o'clock, we adjourned to a restaurant and had dinner and then went up to Dunston and got our luggage away. The Customs made us open our bags and one of mine broke down but after some difficulty we got our luggage to Gateshead station and there I left it with the Steward, who took it home for me for 1/-. I went over to Newcastle then and had an hour and a half in PCWs

[*Pumphrey & Carrick Watson's – see Introduction*]. Jack Logan [*not otherwise identified*] came in and we went and had tea in Grey Street. I saw him off to Heaton and returned to Blackett Street where with T. Smith I visited Allans [*T&G Allan, stationers and booksellers in Blackett St.*] for a few minutes and caught the 6.50 train home.

6 JUNE   Tuesday. I spent a quiet day arranging my clothes and things and developing photos, which came out very well.

7 JUNE   Wednesday. After dinner I went off to Dunston, getting there about twenty to four. The *Salient* was ready to sail and Mrs. Nicholson and Miss were on board. About 4.30 we sailed and had a pleasant trip down despite the cold wind. I found that the steward had deserted, the cook had been promoted, and a new cook telephoned for. On nearing Shields the captain sent me off on the tug to procure kippers and bloaters, which had not arrived. I got warm again in the tug's engine room and one of the men and I hurried ashore and bought kippers – 7/6. We just got on board as the *Salient* entered the piers and I found the other kippers and bloaters had arrived. I shook hands all round where possible and with the Nicholsons quickly boarded the tug and left the *Salient* to steam out into the rough and cold North Sea.

Postscript

Arthur McClelland's subsequent life and career may be briefly sketched. After the voyage he went to work as an 'improver' – the status following apprenticeship (and presumably preceding 'journeyman' and certainly 'master') – with W. Duncan of South Shields, a local grocery chain, also customers of Joshua Wilson & Bros. and therefore well known to his father. Then in the summer of 1907 he opened a shop himself, under the name The City Stores, in a prominent site in Shields Road, a busy shopping street in Byker, east Newcastle. By the first stocktaking some months later he had lost a third of the capital, financed by a loan from his father, but custom quickly built up and by 1913 he had opened four more branches.

The author in later life

When conscription was introduced in 1916, he was not called up for military service – probably, he thought, through being an employer in a vital trade. However, he did not expand the business further (and feared that perhaps he had lost his nerve) until 1921, when he bought W.M. Laws of Gateshead, a firm with nine shops. After some months running the two names in tandem, they were combined into 'Laws Stores' and by 1939 the business had grown to 52 shops.

Also in 1921, his father, Andrew, retired from JWB after 55 years' service. He had served Sunderland as a JP, as a Special Constable in the first world war, and for 26 years as a much esteemed honorary secretary of the Liberal club. Straight after retirement, he set up an office in central Newcastle and bought provisions for both Laws and Duncans, who both marketed 'own-label' goods under the trade name 'Tyne Towns'.

In the 1950s and 1960s Laws was a regional pioneer in converting shops to self-service and opening first-generation supermarkets. In 1985 it was sold to Wm. Low of Dundee, who in 1996 were bought by Tesco. A large portion of the proceeds forms the capital of the Millfield House Foundation (www.mhfdn.org.uk), which applies the income to promote a better society in Tyne and Wear, with special reference to the least fortunate, a cause always close to Arthur McClelland's heart.

The fondness for a telling phrase, evident in the diary, remained with him. In 1919 in writing to his staff, he added to a commonplace injunction his own wittily incontrovertible gloss: 'Serve the customer with a smile – which is as easy as any other way'. In the early 1930s he accepted an invitation to join the Lithosian Society, a Newcastle debating society, and enjoyed preparing for such topics as whether Caesar or Napoleon had been the greater man. Also from the thirties he played a leading role in the Gateshead Rotary Club. After World War II he became a non-executive director of the Northern Counties Building Society, where he was instrumental in the choice of a key chief executive, Fuller Osborn, and played a part in the merger with the Rock, which formed the Northern Rock.

His private life was happy. In 1915 he married Jean Grigor of Stirling, by then a teacher in Newcastle, and they both lived until 1966, the year after their Golden Wedding. He was an early motorist and had the practical and mechanical abilities then so necessary for it. He enjoyed tennis and walking and continued to play chess from time to time with a neighbour. In the 1930s he had a darkroom built in the attic and renewed his amateur developing and printing (by this time, enlarging). I was born in 1922 and was given a happy childhood and a good education – something to which he attached great importance, as the best possible investment for the rest of one's life and work. I had the pleasure of regular and extensive correspondence with him when I was away from Tyneside in the 1940s, and of working with him in the business from 1948. His relations with his daughter-in-law and his four grandchildren were marked by mutual understanding, humour, affection and respect.

A lorry of the firm in 1921 (see pp. 79-80)
Courtesy of TheJournal※ Friday 28 March, 2003

Appendix I
Westolls the shipowners, and the Black Sea trade

> The name – I read it letter by letter on the bow – was James Westoll. Not very romantic, you will say. The name of a very considerable, well-known, and universally respected North country ship-owner, I believe. James Westoll! What better name could an honourable hard-working ship have?
>
> …I followed the James Westoll[1] with my eyes. …she hoisted her flag …the Red Ensign! … the only spot of ardent colour – flame-like, intense… The Red Ensign – the symbolic, protecting, warm bit of bunting flung wide upon the seas, and destined for so many years to be the only roof over my head.
> - *Joseph Conrad (1857-1924)*, <u>A Personal Record</u>, 1912

British vessels were not allowed into the Black Sea until after the Peace of Amiens in 1802, but between 1830 and 1870 trade between the Tyne and the Ukraine, with coal outward and grain back, grew rapidly. During 1831 three sailing ships left the Tyne with coal for Constantinople and the Black Sea, whilst in the third quarter of 1868 ninety vessels left. After the harvest in 1869, 300-400 vessels were reckoned to be heading back with grain.

---

1. The ship so named was built in 1884 whereas this incident is attributable to 1874-75; Conrad, writing much later, must have transferred the owner's name to the ship.

But by sail the outward passage took on average 60 days, and the return was longer, whereas by steam the Salient in 1905, as we have seen, took only 17 days at sea to return to Falmouth. By 1905 commercial sailing ships were a rarity, whereas the steam-driven British merchant navy was at its zenith, accounting for some 40% of world sea-going trade.

James Westoll experienced this revolution. He was born in 1829 in Monkwearmouth, the son of a Master Mariner. After work as a clerk, cashier and shipping agent, by 1863 he had become a junior partner in a shipbroking firm, which became Holmes and Westoll. Its first steamer was launched the following year, and by 1870 the firm had four sailing vessels and six steamers. It then grew rapidly, and on his death in 1895 had 39 steamers under management. He had been an active Scottish Presbyterian throughout his life, and is commemorated in the Monkwearmouth chapel by a marble plaque and stained glass window.

In 1900, then managed by his son and a partner, the firm's 41 steamers were the largest fleet based in Sunderland. Other Westolls vessels sighted from the *Salient* included the *Gerent*, the *Gladys Royle*, the *Lavinia Westoll*, the *Virent* and the *William Middleton* – five out of the ten identified cargo steamers mentioned in the diary. The firm's traffic warranted agents in all the ports visited on this voyage.

The company had long-term contracts with many North East collieries, its main outward cargo at this time being Tyne coal for the expanding railways of Italy and other Mediterranean countries. 'They would then travel up to the Black Sea ports to load grain for the UK and continental ports.' (Alfred Roddenby, *History of James Westoll*, forthcoming). The *Lavinia Westoll* loading manganese ore on April 29, 1905 at Nicolaieff must have been an exception.

It seems clear that the *Salient* left South Shields with a cargo of coal ('shooting into the hold with a hiss and banging') for Genoa. The unloading is not recorded, but the diarist in later life recalled 'coal dust everywhere'. The latter part of the thirteen days in Genoa must have been spent waiting for orders, since they left immediately these came through. Grain was loaded in the Ukraine and that cargo appears to have been for delivery to Rotterdam. At the end of the voyage the ship proceeded up Tyne to Dunston, presumably for another load of coal.

The rest of the twentieth century saw a decline in the Company's business, with vessels lost in the first world war of 1914-18, and the interwar slump, contributing to a steady shrinking of the fleet. The Black Sea trade in 'hard' wheat (suitable for making bread) ended with the first world war and the Russian revolution of 1917 – replaced in due course by wheat from the Baltic (acknowledged in the name of the Baltic flour mill, now an art gallery, on the Gateshead bank of the Tyne) and from the American prairies. The Westoll fleet was then employed mainly in *tramping* and in coal shipments to the continent and along the English coast. The Westoll family sold their interests in 1958, when the company became the Vedra Shipping Co.

Westolls Funnel and Flag

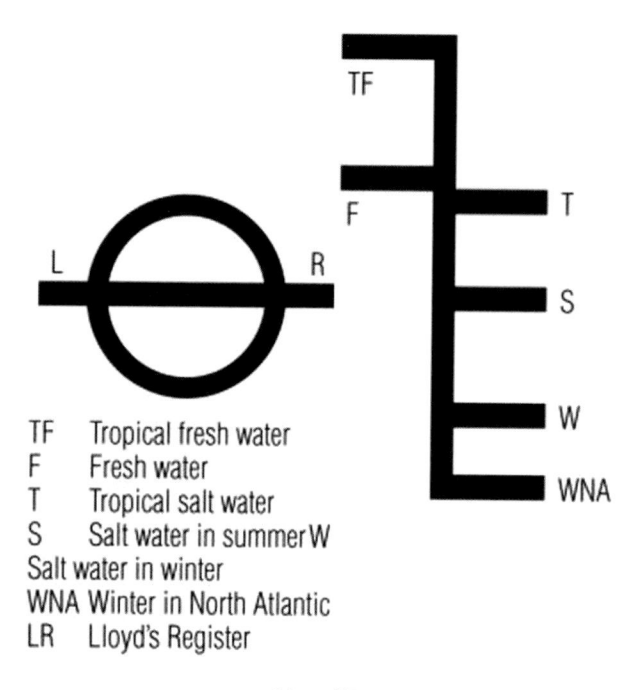

TF   Tropical fresh water
F   Fresh water
T   Tropical salt water
S   Salt water in summer W
Salt water in winter
WNA Winter in North Atlantic
LR   Lloyd's Register

Plimsoll Line

Appendix II
SS Salient, the ship

She was a steel screw-driven two-masted cargo steamship, completed in March 1905 by Short Brothers Ltd. of Sunderland. Her overall length was 356 feet, compared with an average of 321 for the other nine cargo steamers mentioned on the voyage and identified. She was built with an iron division at the centre line, fore and aft, except in the way of hatchways, and with six steel bulkheads and five wood ones. Her total enclosed internal volume available for cargo alone was just over 241,900 cubic feet. Including cargo, bunkers and stores, what she could carry whilst still floating within the Plimsoll requirements[1] (her 'deadweight tonnage') was 6,100 tons. Her draught was 22 ft 2½ in, when loaded to the Plimsoll line maximum for summer

She was designed for the business of carrying Tyne coal out, and Black Sea grain back. Before loading grain the holds had to be swept out and washed down till all trace of coal was eliminated. Many ports had inspectors to check this, and the ship would be held responsible for any contamination of the grain by coal dust.

1. This refers to the requirement to indicate on the ship's side the maximum safe loading levels, or waterline when loaded (see p. 86). The necessary freeboard, or distance between the waterline and the deck, is different for different water densities (sea or fresh) and seasons, being least for tropical fresh water, and most for winter in the north Atlantic. In order to reduce the frequency of accidents, the UK had made showing load lines compulsory in 1876, and fixed the required position of the lines in 1894.

S. S. "SALIENT."

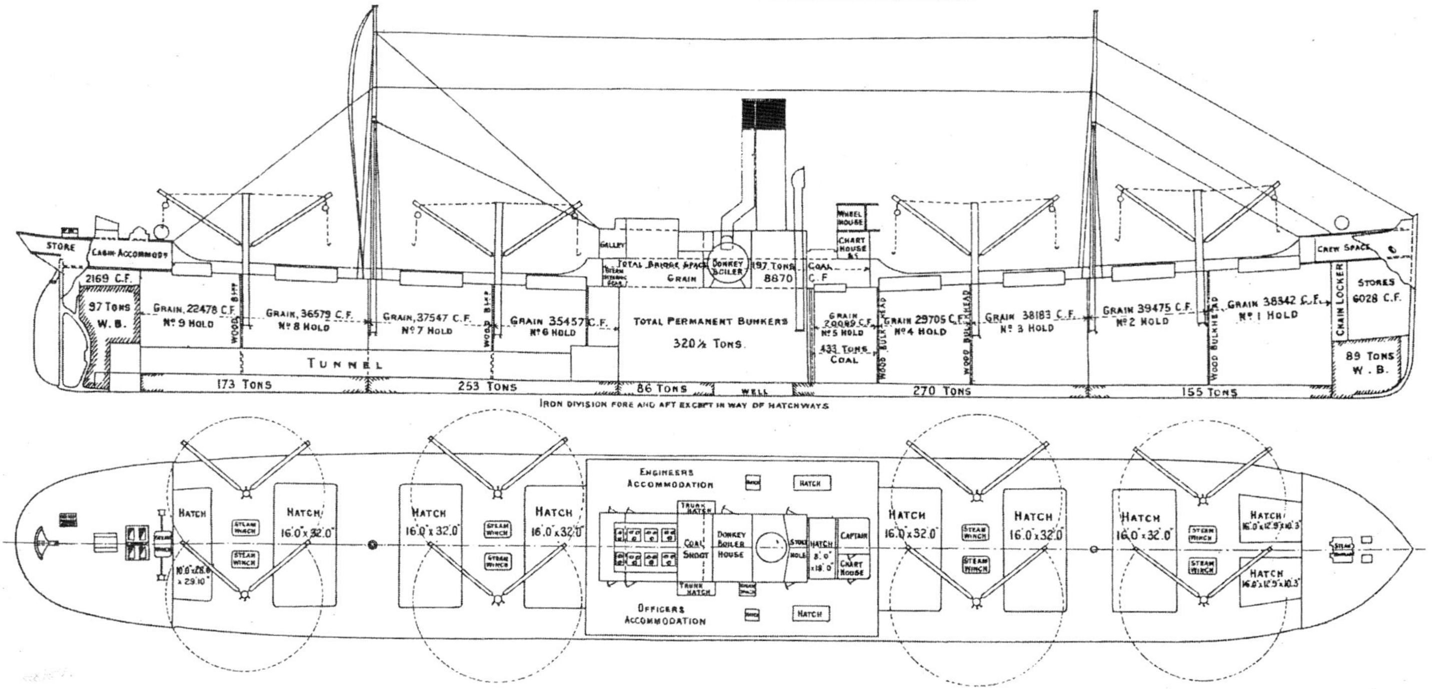

STORE
CABIN ACCOMMODN
2169 C.F.
97 TONS W. B.
GRAIN, 22478 C.F. Nº 9 HOLD
GRAIN, 36579 C.F. Nº 8 HOLD
GRAIN, 37547 C.F. Nº 7 HOLD
GRAIN 35457 C.F. Nº 6 HOLD
TUNNEL
GALLEY
TOTAL BRIDGE SPACE
GRAIN
DONKEY BOILER
197 TONS 8870
COAL C.F.
TOTAL PERMANENT BUNKERS 320½ TONS.
WHEEL HOUSE
CHART HOUSE
GRAIN 20089 C.F. Nº 5 HOLD
433 TONS COAL
WOOD BULKHEAD
GRAIN 29705 C.F. Nº 4 HOLD
GRAIN 38183 C.F. Nº 3 HOLD
GRAIN 39475 C.F. Nº 2 HOLD
GRAIN 38342 C.F. Nº 1 HOLD
CREW SPACE
CHAIN LOCKER
STORES 6028 C.F.
89 TONS W. B.
173 TONS
253 TONS
86 TONS
WELL
270 TONS
155 TONS
IRON DIVISION FORE AND AFT EXCEPT IN WAY OF HATCHWAYS
HATCH 10'0"x28'6" x 29'10"
STEAM WINCH
HATCH 16'0"x32'0"
ENGINEERS ACCOMMODATION
OFFICERS ACCOMMODATION
TRUNK HATCH
COAL SHOOT
DONKEY BOILER HOUSE
STOKE HOLE
HATCH 8'0" x 18'0"
CAPTAIN
CHART HOUSE
HATCH 16'0"x12'9"x10'3"

The drawings (p. 88) show that she had a single funnel amidships; the aft part of it carried the steam from the donkey boiler and the exhaust steam from the ten steam winches. She had masts fore and aft, and 16 *derricks* on eight posts, one of each pair of posts serving the port side and one the starboard side of two adjacent holds. There were nine holds, the fifth from the bow, just forward of the bridge, not being served by the derricks. The total cargo capacity (excluding the *peaks*) was 306,725 cubic feet of grain. (The aft holds tended to have smaller capacity on account of the tunnel to accommodate and allow inspection of the propeller shaft from the engine-room to the stern). The forecastle, bridge deck and poop between them provided another 133 cubic feet of storage.

In addition she carried water ballast, in tanks fore and aft and along her bottom, totalling 1,123 tons, and amidships had permanent bunkers for 320 tons of coal. At 23½ tons per day, enough for 13½ days, at her speed of 9¾ knots. But she may (and for the return from Nikolaieff even to Dartmouth must) have carried extra coal on deck or in an unoccupied hold.

There were six furnaces and two single-ended boilers, yielding a steam pressure of 180 lbs per sq inch. In addition to the driving engines, the steam served ten winches, and the donkey boiler served two ballast engines and two feed engines (to pump feed water to the boilers).

Her engines were made in 1905 by George Clark Ltd. of Sunderland, and were triple expansion (then called tri-compound) engines[2] with cylinder diameters of 24½", 40" and 66" respectively, and 45" length of piston stroke. They generated 1460 effective horsepower, when running at 62 r.p.m. This was designed to yield a speed of 9¾ knots (see p. 93), but actual speed would depend on crew, weather and many other factors. (She raced at 9½ knots (p. 12), fully loaded, to get into Genoa, and at 'eleven knots and over' (p. 32), empty, to get into

2. 'In which the steam expands in three stages in cylinders of increasing diameter to accommodate the increasing volume of the steam' – Collins. There is a fine example in the Discovery Museum, Newcastle.

Constantinople). The table on p. 94 shows her average speed over different stages of the voyage.

> Ten pound was all the pressure then –
> Eh! Eh! – a man wad drive;
> An here, our workin' gauges give one hunder fifty-five!
> We're creepin' on wi' each new rig – less weight an' larger power:
> ……..the tail-rods mark the time,
> The crank-throws give the double bass,
> the feed-pump sobs an' heaves,
> An' now the main eccentrics start their quarrel on the sheaves:
>
> They're all awa! True beat, full power, the clangin' chorus goes
> Clear to the tunnel where they sit, my purring dynamoes.
>
> My seven thousand horse-power here. Eh, Lord!
> They're grand – they're grand!
> – Rudyard Kipling, *M'Andrew's Hymn*, 1896.
>
> [The *Salient* was a smaller ship than this liner for 2,000 'souls aboard', which therefore deployed much greater horsepower. But ten years later, steam pressure had crept up further.]

The elevation shows the holds and other compartments, the derricks and rigging, the rudder and propeller in profile, and the tunnel. It also shows the open wheelhouse above the chart room on the bridge, the crew's quarters forward, cabin accommodation aft, and the galley at the rear of the bridge. The plan shows the range of the derricks in relation to the hatches, the steam winches which drove them, the engineers' and officers' accommodation, and the captain's cabin. She was equipped with steam steering gear, and electric light.

Would she be a 'wet ship'? (see p. 5). Pl. 9 shows considerable water on deck with only a moderate sea. But Richard Keys writes: 'Whether a ship is 'wet' or 'dry' does not usually become apparent until after a few voyages and she has experienced a variety of weather conditions. I can find no evidence to substantiate the statement that 'long' vessels tend to be 'wet', i.e. tend to take on board a lot of water in a seaway. I think it boils

SS Salient crew list
Courtesy of Tyne & Wear Archive Service

down to the design.' The design would include the 'sheer' – 'the upward rise of a ship's deck from amidships towards the stem or stern'. Some sheer is evident from the *Salient's* elevation, and would clearly help during pitching, i.e. rocking between bow and stern.

The Crew List (p. 91) shows that the *Salient's* crew on 8 March 1905 numbered 28. The Master (£25 a month), mate (£12) and 2nd mate (£9), between them provided the management and navigation. The 1st, 2nd, 3rd, and 4th engineers at £16, £12, £8, and £7 respectively, with a donkeyman and six firemen or trimmers, ensured the motive power. The bo'sun, assisted by four able seamen, one ordinary seaman, J. Bullock, and four apprentices (unpaid save for board and keep and the benefit of experience), doubtless covered all work on deck at sea and in port. Finally there was a steward, cook and carpenter. The total came to £167 16s 0d a month, for a voyage which lasted just under three months. Advance notes (p. 1) totalling £15, for half (in one case more) of the wage were given to some of the seamen and all but one of the engineers. 'Allotments' of around half were given to the steward, cook, carpenter and bo'sun, and to the engineers and donkeyman, The two passengers had nominal roles (Arthur McClelland 1/- as purser), and one Jose Ferrier appears to have been paid £2 5s 0d at Genoa.

She sailed again on June 7, with in large part the same crew. A. Reed, the cook, had become steward (see p.77), one of the able seamen had been replaced, three of the six trimmers had also changed, and of course she was without her two former passengers. The *Salient* herself continued in service with James Westoll (changed to Westoll Steamships in 1929) until 1935, when she was sold to shipowners in Cardiff and by them to a shipbreaking company in Blyth, for breaking up to take advantage of the government's 'scrap and build' scheme.

Appendix III

Distances and speed

The following table gives distances travelled at sea, times taken, and consequent speed in knots. The distances in heavy type are mainly taken from 'Distances Between Ports' and are steaming distances (for example allowing for detours to avoid sandbanks) in nautical miles. Other distances are estimated roughly from maps, converted to nautical miles.

The times are calculated from references in the diary to when the *Salient* reached or left ports, and when landmarks were sighted. The times recorded would have been 'ship times', probably set by changing clocks at night by 20 minutes when necessary. Solar time at the eastern end of the voyage would have been two hours later than in the west. Taking account of this would very slightly increase eastbound speeds and reduce westbound.

The (1905) quoted design speed of the *Salient* was 9¾ knots, assuming that the ship is 'loaded, with a clean bottom' (the drag exerted by barnacles, etc., can reduce speed). One nautical mile, as agreed at the Monaco international conference of 1929, equals 1,825 metres, which is just over 1.15 miles. (Since the UK did not adopt the Monaco convention until 1970, the figure of 9¾ may be very slightly over-stated in present-day terms).

Despite rough-and-ready measurement of distances, variations in the speed mainly reflect whether or not the ship was full of cargo, and reported weather conditions. By the end of the voyage, 1039 hours or 43¼ days had been spent at sea (including the

Bug and Dnieper rivers, and between the Hook and Rotterdam), and 7991 nautical miles (9185 land miles) covered, at an average speed of 7.7 knots.

Stage	Distance, nautical miles	Time, hours	Knots	Notes
From Tyne to Flamborough Head	74	9.5	7.8	1
…to Cross Sands	117	15	7.8	
…to St. Catherine's Point	290	34.5	8.4	
…to C. Finistere	499	157	3.2	2
Tyne to C. Finistere	**980**	222.5	**4.4**	
…to Gibraltar	**537**	60	**8.95**	
…to Genoa	**848**	91.5	**9.3**	
Tyne to Genoa	**2365**	333	**7.1**	
…to Messina	442	50	8.8	3
…to 'Old Man's Corner'	434	47.5	9.1	3
…to Constantinople	434	41	10.6	3
Genoa to Constantinople	**1310**	138.5	**9.5**	3
…to Kherson	**400**	40	**10**	3
Kherson to Nicolaieff	60	8.5	**7.1**	
…to Constantinople	**398**	50	**8.0**	
…to Pantellaria	835	108	7.7	
…to Gibraltar	870	98	8.9	
Constantinople to Gibraltar	**1780**	208	**8.6**	
…to Cape St, Vincent	174	37	4.7	
…to Cape Finistere	245	39	6.2	
…to Dartmouth	470	73	6.4	4
…to Dover	300	21	12.4	5
…to Hook	120	11	10.9	5
…to Rotterdam	**19**	2.25	8.4	
…to Hook	**19**	2.25	8.4	3
…to Tyne	**281**	76.5	**10.6**	3
Total	**7991**	1039	**7.7**	

Notes:

1. Assuming the same speed north of Flamborough Head as in the next leg.

2. Head winds and high seas. Hove to for much of 15 March. Captain reckoned to have lost three days by 19 March. Weather charts held at the National Meteorological Archive, Exeter, indicate that the period around 15 March was particularly stormy, with severe gales from the South-south-west across the Bay of Biscay.
3. Sailing empty.
4. See note (2). Similar charts for the period around 22nd May indicate strong to gale force winds across the Bay of Biscay from the North-east.
5. Mileage (e.g. taking account of shipping lanes) probably underestimated.

Appendix IV
Currency and prices

The diarist frequently notes – sometimes in the local currency and sometimes in sterling – how much he was asked, or paid, for articles or services ashore. In 1905, £1 sterling would buy nearly ten Russian roubles, about twelve Netherlands guilders, or 25 French francs (prices in Genoa are quoted in francs, but a French franc then had the same value as an Italian lira).

But that £1 was worth much more than £1 today. To give any contemporary meaning to these figures is a difficult task, and many of the difficulties are insoluble – you are just not comparing like with like. However, combining indices for 1905-13 and for 1913-2005, we may say that consumer prices in those hundred years have risen by 78 times, that a sovereign then would have bought as much as £78 today, or conversely that the value of the currency has fallen, and £1 from 1905 (as distinct, of course, from the gold in a 1905 sovereign) would buy only as much as the equivalent of 1.28p. in today's currency.

The prices quoted may also be compared with the monthly pay for each member of the crew, given in the Crew List (p. 91). This ranges from £25 for the master to £4 10s 0d for able seamen and firemen. Adjusting for the subsequent inflation, the captain was receiving the purchasing power of £450 a week, and an AB that of £81, a ratio of 5.5 to 1. Board and lodging were of course provided in addition, but on the other hand, crew members were in some respects working, in today's phrase, '24/7' weeks.

Appendix V
List of characters mentioned by name

Members of the ship's company (see also p. 91)
The captain, George Nicholson. Born in Evesham but served his apprenticeship with Adamson of Sunderland, and then joined Westolls. He had previously commanded the *James Cameron* (1888-91), the *George Royle* and the *Virent*. In 1911 he was appointed Marine Superintendent, serving in that post until his death at home in Roker, Sunderland, in 1934.

Arthur Newton, Mate
Alf Alderson, 2nd Mate
G. E. Brown, Steward, 'a handy man and is surgeon as well'.
'Chips' = ship's carpenter, Orston Watt
Mr. Cumming ('C'), the other passenger. An elderly man who fell ill in Nikolaieff and was put ashore in Constantinople on the way back.

Other Westolls seafarers
Captain James William Stephenson of Westolls. Born Monkwearmouth, 1867; Masters Certificate, S. Shields, 1893. Present during the trials, and came overland to meet the *Salient* at Genoa. Met it also at Rotterdam, returning by the Harwich ferry. Presumably temporarily at head office before taking up captaincy of the *Gladys Royle* (though the diary names that as his ship during his visit to Genoa). This was his seventh (out of ten) vessel with Westolls.

Captain Mark Anthony Ramshaw of Westolls. Born Sunderland, 1869; Masters Certificate, Sunderland, 1893. The *Munificent* was the sixth of nine Westolls ships which he captained.
Mr. Matthew Hodgson, 34, Mate of the *Lavinia Westoll*, later a Westolls captain.
Mr. Short, Chief Engineer of the *Lavinia Westoll*.
Mr. Philpot, 2nd Engineer of the *Lavinia Westoll*.
3rd Engineer, the *Lavinia Westoll*.
William Payne, passenger on the *Lavinia Westoll*.
Captain Marshall. Possibly Westolls. Referred to only on 1 May.

Landbased Westolls employees or agents
J. White, Westolls agent in Genoa.
Steingart, in the office of the Westolls agent in Kherson, Sidney Reed & Co.
Mr. Gallager and Mr. Fleming, presumably with Westolls Odessa agents McNabbs.
Mr. Swan, Westolls agent in Constantinople.

Local people met in Ukraine
Mr. N. A. Baltjansky. English-speaking shopkeeper in Kherson.
'Jenny', eighteen-year-old daughter of beekeeper at Nikolaieff.
Rosenberg, a Jewish banker and his wife in Nikolaieff.
Mickaelaeff, another Jewish family in Nikolaieff.
'Helene', 'the captain's great favourite', visited the *Salient* at Nikolaieff.

Others
Captain Donaldson. Well known and characterful Bosporus pilot. Willie and Jack, the diarist's younger brothers. They studied (respectively, marine architecture and marine engineering) at Armstrong College, later Newcastle University. Both later served with the merchant marine (and Jack the RN), Willie afterwards being responsible for a number of engineering inventions including a ship's davit, and Jack serving as an inspector of lighthouses for Trinity House.

T. Smith, presumably a fellow apprentice of A. McC. 'Thos Smith' appears among 28 signatures on the front endpapers of one of the three India-paper volumes of Shakespeare's works, 'Presented by staff of T. Carrick Watson & Son when A. McC finished his apprenticeship in February 1905'.

Appendix VI

Other vessels identified

Where identified, entries give gross tonnage, place and year of completion, yard; owners. This is followed by any other information. Steam cargo vessels unless otherwise indicated. Alphabetical order for those identified, other references follow.

Bencliffe, 2210, Sunderland 1894, Doxford; Horsley Line, West Hartlepool. Acquired by German owners, 1913; reparation to UK, 1920; again German, 1922; sold for breaking up, 1931.

Britannia (HMS), 3994. Battleship. Portsmouth Dockyard 1860, as *Prince of Wales*. Reduced to training duties 1869, broken up at Blyth 1916.

Cardiff Castle. Not in register.

Elswick Tower, 3923, Newcastle 1901, R. Stephenson; Elswick Shipping; Greek owner 1930, broken up 1932.

Gerent, 2283, Sunderland 1888, Short Bros; Westolls; broken up at Blyth, 1928.

Gladys Royle, 3287, Sunderland 1894, Short Bros; Westolls. Captured and sunk with explosive charges by German sailing ship (!) raider *Seeadler* (Sea Eagle), near Azores, 1917.

Hohenzollern, 4200, 1923. German royal yacht for Kaiser Wilhelm II. Crew 295, maximum speed 21.5 knots, range 2000 sea miles, withdrawn 1923.

Lavinia Westoll, 3151, Sunderland 1895, Short Bros; Westolls; Sunk 1916 by mine laid by U-boat UC6 near Spurn, bound with iron ore for Tees from Almeria.

Munificent. Destroyed at Scarborough by German raid in late 1914 or early 1915.

Ormuz, 6031, Glasgow 1887, Fairfield; Orient; French 1912, broken up 1922.

Princess Heinrich. See p. 60 and pl. 30

Roma, 3634, Sunderland 1901, J. L. Thompson; Rowland & Marwood, Whitby. Greek from 1923 till broken up 1952.

Tregarthen, 2171, South Shields 1904, Redheads; Hain Steamship Co, St. Ives; later French, Greek, Finnish owners, torpedoed and sunk by U-boat U37 off Finisterre, bound from Greenock to Dakar.

Virent, 3771 Sunderland 1902, Osbourne Graham. Westolls. Italian 1927, broken up 1932.

William Middleton (not Mydaleton), 2539. Sunderland 1893, Short Bros; Westolls; Italian 1927, broken up 1932.

Appendix VII

Glossary

See reference in Editor's Note, p. xi. Definitions in quotation marks are from Collins English Dictionary, 3rd edition 1991.

Advance Note A note from the company to a seaman, promising to pay him or his nominee a portion of the wages due for the voyage, within a certain time after he has sailed. Thus a wife could draw on her husband's earnings before he returned.

B/L, or Bill of Lading Statement of cargo taken on board, signed by the master as acceptance of safe delivery.

Boatswain, or Bosun 'A petty officer … responsible for maintenance of the ship and its equipment'.

Boom 'A beam or spar, qv, pivoting at the foot of the mast of a derrick, qv, controlling the distance from the mast at which a load is lifted or lowered'. Cf. jib

Cargo 'jumping' An arrangement whereby four or five seamen, each holding a rope attached to the same load, simultaneously jump from the tops of step-ladders, thus tipping heavy cargo into a container on land, or into a hold. See much fuller description in Richard E. Keys, *The Sailing Ships of Aln and Coquet*, 1993, pp. 6-7.

Chart House A room below the wheel house where charts are stored and chart work carried out. See p. 88 and pl. 7.

Coalhulk see 'Hulk'.

Come off (*Counter-intuitively*) to board, come on board.

Companion 'A raised frame on an upper deck with windows to give light to the deck below'.

Deadlight A shutter for sealing off a porthole.

Derrick A simple crane having lifting tackle slung from a boom, qv.

Dinner The midday meal, as in Northern English usage. Cf. 'tea'; ('Supper' is mentioned on p. 2; however this was clearly nearing midnight).

Donkey engine 'A small auxiliary engine', for example used to transmit the movement of the wheel in the wheel house; see 'rod and chain'.

Drosky or droshky 'An open four-wheeled horse-drawn passenger carriage, formerly used in Russia'.

Eccentric rod A device for converting rotary motion to reciprocating motion (so, with cam, the opposite to a connecting rod and crankshaft).

Fiddle A small railing fitted around the top of a table to prevent objects falling off it in bad weather.

Flint striker A hand-held device to produce a spark, e.g. for lighting gas, by striking a flint against a rough metal surface.

GRT, Gross Register Tonnage Represents the total internal volume of a vessel, with some exemptions for non-productive spaces such as crew quarters. One gross register ton is equal to a volume of 100 cubic feet (2.83 m^3).

Harness cask A tub, usually conical in shape, for stowing the salt provisions in current use.

Hulk 'The body of an abandoned vessel' or 'the frame or hull of a ship, used as a storehouse, etc.'

Jib 'The projecting arm of a crane or the boom, qv, of derrick, qv, especially one that is pivoted to enable it to be raised or lowered'. Cf. boom.

Knots Sea miles per hour; one sea mile = about 1.15 statute miles or 1.85 km.

Lazaretto 'A storeroom between decks of a ship' – for provisions.

Lead 'A lead weight suspended on a line used to take soundings of the depth of water'. **Heave the lead** Drop such a line for this purpose.

Lead line A length of line, marked at various points in multiples of fathoms, for taking soundings and thus ascertaining the depth of water below the ship and taking a sample of the bottom.

Peak 'The extreme forward (forepeak) or aft (afterpeak) part of the hull.'

Poop A raised structure at the stern of a vessel.

Pratique Formal permission given to a vessel to use a foreign port upon satisfying the requirements of local health authorities.

Rod and chain The method of linking the donkey engine (qv) to the rudder; over the deck, rods (in channels) were used for straight stretches, linked by chains where a change of direction was required (see pl. 8, lower left corner).

Separation cloths Sheets of a coarse material such as burlap, used to separate different cargos, e.g. different types of grain.

Staithes (normally in plural) A construction whereby railway wagons can be moved above moored ships and drop their load into chutes or direct into the holds, by the wagon bottom being opened.

Sounding hole A vertical tube from above deck to the ship's hull through which a lead line can be dropped to ascertain the depth of water in the bilge and take a sample of it.

Spar 'Any piece of nautical gear resembling a pole, and used as a mast, boom (qv), gaff, etc.'.

Tea The evening meal. Cf. 'dinner'.

Thrust The engine imparts rotary motion through the propeller shaft to the propeller, which pushes the water back, thus providing forward thrust, which however has to be delivered not to the engine but to the ship as a whole. This is achieved through the thrust bearing, 'a low-friction bearing on a rotating shaft that resists axial thrust in the shaft. Usually it consists of a collar which bears against a ring', the ring being firmly anchored to the ship. A single bearing could contain five pairs of collars and rings, the 'rings' being in the shape of a horse-shoe, facing downwards. The thrust must be sufficient to displace the water moved aside (equal to the weight of the ship plus that of its entire load) as the ship moves forward.

Tramping Carrying cargo wherever each shipper desires, rather than running between ports on a schedule.

Trimmer A fireman employed in moving coal to ensure that after loading, or as it is used up, the load is properly balanced.

Tunnel A passage running from the engine-room to near the propeller, containing the propeller shaft and giving access to it. (See also pp. 30 and 88).

Turks head An ornamental turban-like knot made by weaving small cord round a larger rope.

Windlass 'A machine for raising weights by winding a rope or chain upon a barrel or drum driven by a crank, motor, etc.'

Index

A
abacus 42
Ackworth School 8, 20
advance notes 1, 92
Alderson, 2nd mate 2, 43, 49
Alexander Park 52
Alexandra, Queen of Britain xv, 25n, pl.21
Alexandra, Tsarina of Russia 54n
Alexandra column 52
architecture,
    leisure interest at school 73
    at Antwerp zoo 74
Armenians, attacks on 33n
    to be seen in Constantinople 59
    boys, school for 35n
Atlantic 5, 64, 87n

B
Balearic Islands 10
Batoum, oil tankers bound for 32
battleships, at Genoa 12
    Turkey's fleet of six 32
    at Dartmouth, for training 67, pl.31
    at target practice 68
    Belgian 74
bazaar 58
Bevin, Ernest xviii

birthday, author's 8
    Czarina's 54
Biscay, Bay of, outward passage 7
    Golfe du Lion worse than 11
    return passage 65
    weather data 95
Black Sea xiii, 30, 37, 47, 50, 55, 56n, 63
    explosion on ship in 50
    the trade with 84-87
boat drill 62, 65, pl.11
bortsch 46
Bosporus 33, 34, 35, 56, 59
boules 20
Bret Harte, author 40
bridges, extemporised 7
Bug, River 37, 38, 47, 94

C
camera 7, 10n, 29, 55, 57, 58, 73
    detained at sites 19, 23
    sealed at customs 38
    improperly fastened 29
car, *see also* 'tram'
    in Genoa, 16, 20-22
    in Nikolaieff 49
Carthagena 10
Cathedral, in Genoa 16
    in Antwerp 73-74, pl.40

cavalry 51
Cerigo 60
chart house, captain sleeps in 6
   pillows for chronometer 42
   clerical job by diarist 62
chess 7, 9, 10, 20, 29, 30, 32, 55, 62, 63, 65
   board, painted on table 9, pl.13
   play prevented by rolling 8
   captain shouting 'bad move' 9
   games captain lost
     against captain of
     Elswick Tower 38
   playing without bishop 62, 63, 65
   through 'sea fever' 66
   trying to read newspaper 60
   game with Cummins 36
   in later life 80
Chief (Engineer) 6, 30, 31, 39, 43, 45, 49, 50, 54, 62, 65, 66, 69, 76, 92, pl. 18
Cirito 31
Clyde 34
Columbus 19, 22
Conrad, Joseph, quoted 83
Constantinople, race to reach 32
   seen from ship 33-34, 56
   saved by dogs 34
   ferries to Scutari 34
   exploring the city 57-59
cranes 12
Crete 55, 60
Crew List, variety of skills xv
   facsimile 91
   German fireman 41
   pay due 76
   summarised 92
   pay rates 97
cribbage 54, 62, 63, 65

cricket 5, 20, 42, 43, 44
Crimea 34
Cross Sands 4, 94
Cummings, C, or 'the old man'
   first impression 2
   seeing Genoa with diarist 16-25
   dressed as baker 36, pl.15
   joke played on 35
   low view of 'the modern traveller' 21, 31, 44
   unwell 30, 40, 43, 53
   put ashore at Constantinople 57
Customs xv
   sealing up at Genoa 11, 13
   severity in Russia 36
   at Dartmouth 67
   at Dunston 76
Czarina 54

D

Dardanelles xv, 31-32, 60
Dartmouth xv, 66, 67, 89, 94
deadlight 7, pl.16
Deal 5
deck, all hands on 38, 48, 55
   walking the 11
   seas over lower 3, 5, 6, 7, pl.9
   deck chairs 26, 29, pl.12, 14
diamond ring, possibly a reward for saving a life 8
Dnieper, River 37, 38, 94
Dog's Isle 34
Donaldson (pilot) 56, 100
Dunston (on Tyne) 3, 76, 77, 85

E

Easter 43, 48, 49
Egyptian column 58
Eisenstein, Sergei 48
elevators (grain) 40, 48
Elswick (Newcastle) 56

SS Elswick Tower 38-44
Empress of Germany 13
engine(s), stopped 4, 7
    at full speed 11
    visit to engine-room 30
    giving trouble 59
    specifications 89
Erthogroul (Sultan's yacht) 56, pl.25
Europe, largest wooden
   structure in 3, pl.41
    where Turks first crossed into 56
    most southerly point 62

F

Fat Mary, washerwoman, purser's role
   in getting her ashore 40
    disproved suspicions 43
fiddles (for meals) 6, 7, 30
Finisterre 8, 94
Fischers 53
fishing fleet 4, 10, 68
flag, yellow 12
   house 65
    Westolls (depicted) 85
Fleming 51-52, 100
football 20-21, 43, 44, 49
francs 16, 22, 97
funicular 23

G

Galata Bridge 57, 58-59
Gallipoli xv, 32, 60
Gatta 10
geese 32
Genoa, arrival 12
   character 15
   exploring 16-26
   map 18
German fireman 41
   -speaking 53
   fate of British ships 103-104

Germany, Empress of xv, 13, pl.20
Gibraltar 9, pl.27, 64, 94
Golfe du Lion 11
Goodwin Sands 5, 68
Great Yarmouth 4
Greece 31, 60
Greenwich Mean Time 13, 73

H

Hamburg 29, 68
hatches 12, 31, 62, 90
Helene (Mickaelaieff) 50
Hepburn, Prof. Tony *xiii*
Hohenzollern 13, pl.20, 103
Howard, John, commemorated 42,
   pl.22, 23
hubble-bubbles 59
Hume, Fergus, author 43

I

Isle of Wight, sighted 5, 68, pl.5

J

Jennie, captain's favourite 50, 54
Jewish 41, 48-49, 100
Jonah, on board? 6
Joshua Wilson & Brothers xv

K

Keys, Richard xii, 90, 105
Kherson, description 37-38
   experiences in 36-45
   last sight of 48
Khios 31
Kipling, Rudyard, quoted 90
kopek 49, 54
Koran 57, 58

L

Lambert, Mrs. Clare xii
Lazaretto 53
lightship 4, 68, 69

live stock 55

M
Manasaus 54
Marmora 32, 33, 60
Masefield, John, quoted xiii
massacres of 1894, seen by steward, reported in Mobile, Al 33
Matapan 62
Mazzini 23, 24, 26
McClelland, Andrew Penman xv
    Arthur ix, x, xv, 9, 79-81, 92
    Grigor x, xii
    Jack 2, 76, 100
    Willie 2, 76, 100
McNabb 51
Masefield, John, quoted xiii
Mecca 58
Meldrum, Mr. 2
Messageries Maritimes 9, 32
Messina 30, 94
Mickaelaeff, family in Nikolaieff 50
Mill Dam, S. Shields 1, 3, 76, pl.2
Milton, John, quoted xv
minarets 33, 34, 56
Monaco 11
Monte Cristo 29
mosque 57, 58
Mouyiloff 53
muezzins 34

N
Newcastle xv, xvi, 2, 9, 51n, 56n, 76, 79, 80n
Newton (Mate) 26, 49, 76, 99
Nice 11, 24, 25, 68
Nicholson, Captain (otherwise 'the captain', *passim*) 1, pl.8, 8, 20, 24, 53, 56, 59, 69, 73, 77, 99
Nightingale, Florence 34

O
Ochikoff 36-38, 47, 55
Odessa xv, 27, 40, Hotel O. 45
    described 47-48, visited 51-52, 55
Olga, attraction at milk shop 49
Orient (shipping line) 10
Ormuz (ship) 10
Ottoman Empire xvii

P
P&O 9, 10
Paginini 22
Palace 19, 26, 34, 72, 75
pashas 58
Passover 41, 42, 48, 51
Paul 24
Pegli 23
Pera 57, 58
photographs 10, 25, 26
Point Malla 60
poop 5, 6, 7, 30, 35, 39, 42, 44, 48, 60, 63, 89, pl.6, 8, 12, 14
Porpoises 32, 65
Portuguese 8
postcards 17, 51, 54, 58, 67, 73
pratique 12, 32, 33
Princess Heinrich 25, 68, 104, pl.30
propeller 3, 38, 89, 90
Protection and Indemnity Clubs 39n
Pumphrey & Carrick Watson xv, 77
purser 40, 48, 92

Q
Quaker 8n

R
Ramshaw 22- 26, 31
Riviera 11, 12, 68
Robert College 33n
Roddenby, Alfred xii, 84

Rosenberg 50, 51
Rotterdam xv, 66, 69-75, 94
 map of visits from 70
Russia xvii, Ch. 4, 5
Russian
 Westoll agent 39
 cigarettes 40
 sentry 41
 'nye ponomayoo' 41
 a R. dinner 45
 carts 45
 transliteration 45n.
 Easter 48 & n.
 a R. house 50
 1917 revolution 85
 roubles 97
Russians, at Ochikoff 38
 singing 40
 illiteracy 41
 attempting to detect 48

S

SS Salient on voyage 3-77
 description 87-90
 plans 88
 speeds 92-95
 saloon 4, 5, 9, pl.13
San Remo 11
Santa Sofia 57, 59, pl.26
Savona 24, 25
Scarlet Fever 31
Scutari 34
Seagulls 6, 66
Seaman's Institute 16
Seaton Sluice 3
sentry 41
separation cloths 53
Seraglio 33, 34
Sidney Reed & Company 45
Sierra Nevada 10
South Shields xv, 1, 3, 76, 79, 84

St. Catherine's Point 5, 68, pl.5
St. Mary's Island 3
St. Vincent 9, 55, 65
staithes 3, pl.41
stamps 16, 17, 71
Steingart 45
Stephenson, Captain 13, 22, 71, 75, pl.12
steward 1-7, 11, 33, 34, 39, 40, 45, 76-77, 92
Stromboli 30
Sultana 33
Sunderland xv, 2, 4, 63, 71, 76, 80, 84, 87, 89, 92, 93
Swan 35, 56, 57, 59
Synagogue 42

T

Tenedos 32, 60, pl.24
Terifa 9
thrust 30
tide 2, 5, 39, 69, 76
torpedo boat 4, 64
tram, *see also* 'car' 9, 41, 49, 51, 72, 74-75
Tregarthen 39
trials 2-4, 13
trimmer 31, 92
tunnel (for propellor shaft) 30, 57, 88, 89, 90
Turk, Turkey, Turkish 31-33, 42, 56-59, 60
Tyne ix, xii, xiii, 3, 76, 80, 83-85, 87, 94

V

Ventnor 5
Victoria, Queen of Britain 58

W

wave 6, 8, 51, 66
Westolls 49, 66, 67, 70, 90, 92

history 84-86
insignia 86
White, J 23
wind 4-11, 31-33, 39, 40, 44,
  66-67, 75, 77, 95
Wrigglesworth, Sir Ian ix, xii

Y
Yacht Club 55
Yildiz Kiosk 57

Publications

The Jarrow Crusade: Protest and Legend
by Matt Perry   ISBN 1873757- 60-3   **Price: £12.95**

The Jarrow Crusade is hailed as a defining moment of the hungry thirties. It was the protest of the people of a Tyneside town against the closure of their shipyard and the blocking of their new steelworks. More than any other protest, it is held up as a model for others to follow. Its rejection of politics and its courting of respectable opinion are seen as the reason for its success; this at least is the version of events that many will be familiar. However, the Crusade did not win jobs for Jarrow and a series of myths and folklore have come to surround the event. This book is an attempt to get to grips with the real history of the Crusade. It is a history that offers insights into the character of British society and into the nature of protest then and now.

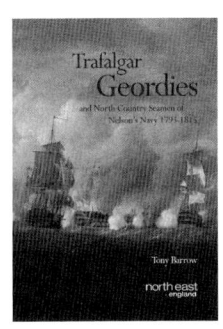

Trafalgar Geordies and North Country Seamen of Nelson's Navy 1793-1815
by Tony Barrow   ISBN 1905438-00-1   **Price: £11.95**

Few of the memorable naval episodes in British history before the twentieth century were recorded from the perspective of the common seaman despite their vital contribution to the victories of British fleets abroad. At the end of the eighteenth century the maritime communities of North East England, from Berwick to Whitby, contained one of the most important concentrations of skilled mariners anywhere in the United Kingdom. These seamen were prime targets for the press gang and few of them escaped the obligation to use their seafaring skills manning the warships of Nelson's navy. These men served with distinction in every major naval engagement of the Napoleonic era. The battle of Trafalgar in 1805 represented the culmination of their achievement. Seamen from North East England, over 500 in total, served in the crews of every ship that fought with Nelson that day.

The Whaling Trade of North-East England 1750-1850
by Tony Barrow   ISBN 1 873757 83 2   **Price: £12.95**

North East England was one of the most important centres of British whaling enterprise. From Berwick in the north to Whitby in the south, stoutly built whaling ships sailed annually to the Arctic grounds in search of the Greenland whale. The Whaling Trade of North-East England 1750-1850, is the first comprehensive, academic account of this fascinating aspect of the maritime heritage of the region.

Sir Tom Cowie A True Entrepreneur – A Biography
by Denise Robertson – Foreword by Wilbur Smith
Hardback – ISBN 1 873757 30 1   *Price: £16.99*
Paperback – ISBN 1 873757 84 0   *Price: £8.99*

This is the storey of a young man from Sunderland who was discharged from the RAF in 1946 with a gratuity and went on to build one of the fastest-growing companies in the United Kingdom. The story moves from the small backyard where Tom Cowie's motor-cycle business started, through his days as manager and director of a successful lease-hire car company, to his accolades for political and other services.

Tom Hadaway The Prison Plays
*Including Long Shadows co-written with Pauline Hadaway,
Edited and with an introduction by Val McLane*
ISBN 1 873757 10 7   *Price: £12.95 Now: £9.95*

Tom Hadaway is one of North East England's leading playwrights. He has written more than twenty plays, films and television scripts, including The Filleting Machine, God Bless Thee Jackie Maddison, Seafarers and The Long Line, all performed by The Live Theatre in Newcastle. The Prison Plays is a collection of two full-length and two short plays written after his term as writer in residence at Durham and Frankland prisons in 1986.

Britain and the Baltic Studies in Commercial, Political and Cultural Relations 1500-2000
Edited by Tony Barrow and Patrick Salmon
ISBN 1873757 49 2   *Price: £17.95 Now: £9.95*

Political, commercial and cultural connections between Britain and the Baltic are amongst the oldest and most enduring in the historical record. And yet, paradoxically, they are also amongst the least known and poorly understood. The essays contained within this volume demonstrate that scholarly study of Britain's historical relationship with the countries of Scandinavia and the Baltic region is both varied and dynamic.

Art & the Spiritual *Edited by Bill Hall and David Jasper*
ISBN 1 873757 78 6   *Price: £14.95 Now: £9.95*

A collection of essays and responses; this book is challenging without retreating into the arcane world of academic debate and discussion. Written by artists, each essay is given a response by a professional theologian.

To order any of the above publications you can either Fax, Telephone or contact: Business Education Publishers Limited, The Teleport, Doxford International, Sunderland, SR3 3XD,
Tel: +44(0) 191 5252410, Fax: +44(0) 191 5201815, email: info@bepl.com